AND JUSTICE FOR SOME

AND
JUSTICE FOR SOME

An Exposé of the Lawyers and Judges
Who Let Dangerous Criminals Go Free

WENDY MURPHY

SENTINEL

SENTINEL
Published by the Penguin Group

Penguin Group (USA) Inc., 375 Hudson Street, New York, New York 10014, USA • Penguin Group (Canada), 90 Eglinton Avenue East, Suite 700, Toronto, Ontario M4P 2Y3, Canada (a division of Pearson Penguin Canada Inc.) • Penguin Books Ltd, 80 Strand, London WC2R 0RL, England • Penguin Group Ireland, 25 St. Stephen's Green, Dublin 2, Ireland (a division of Penguin Books Ltd) • Penguin Group (Australia), 250 Camberwell Road, Camberwell, Victoria 3124, Australia (a division of Pearson Australia Group Pty Ltd) • Penguin Books India Pvt. Ltd, 11 Community Centre, Panchsheel Park, New Delhi – 110 017, India • Penguin Group (NZ), 67 Apollo Drive, North Shore 0745, Auckland, New Zealand (a division of Pearson New Zealand Ltd) • Penguin Books (South Africa) (Pty) Ltd, 24 Sturdee Avenue, Rosebank, Johannesburg 2196, South Africa

Penguin Books Ltd, Registered Offices: 80 Strand, London WC2R 0RL, England

First published in 2007 by Sentinel, a member of Penguin Group (USA) Inc.

10 9 8 7 6 5 4 3 2 1

LIBRARY OF CONGRESS CATALOGING IN PUBLICATION DATA
Murphy, Wendy, 1960–
And justice for some : an expose of the lawyers and judges who let dangerous criminals go free / Wendy Murphy.
    p. cm.
Includes index.
ISBN 978-1-59523-036-2
1. Criminal justice, Administration of—United States. I. Title.
KF9223.Z9M87 2007
345.73'05—dc22   2007001919

Printed in the United States of America
Designed by Spring Hoteling • Set in Adobe Garamond

To all the victims, win or lose, who fought for justice.
And to the silent ones who didn't
even try because they had no faith.

FOREWORD

Most of us have heard the term Crusader for Justice, and that is
what Wendy Murphy is. Trying to reform the American justice
system so that regular folks have a shot at some kind of fair play
is a full-time job; one that is frustrating, sometimes maddening.
The no-spin reason is that the United States is no longer a country that can tout "and justice for all." Now the legal system is
Las Vegas, a game of chance, a roll of the dice. Even if you have
been gravely wronged, the system may let you down big time.
That's why you need to read this book.

Money, of course, is the root of all legal evil. The more you
can spend, the more lawyers you can hire, the more "experts"

you can buy to tell the jury things that will bewilder them, the more private investigators you can hire to dig up dirt on your legal opponents. But if you are short of cash, watch out. The legal system is not a place where the poor are well accommodated.

So the deck is stacked from the start. Wealthy Americans have a much greater chance not only to get justice, but also to avoid justice. In a country that has declared "all men are created equal," there is something deeply disturbing about that.

In the upcoming pages, Wendy Murphy will walk us through what the American justice system has devolved into. She will introduce us to judges intoxicated by power, lawyers who put money above honesty, jurors who just want to go home and will violate their consciences to do so. But the book also offers solutions and a call for reform. I mean what kind of country are we if we allow children and the elderly to be brutalized with little consequence? If we accept a legal system that has allowed itself to spiral out of control so that its participants can get rich and powerful.

Through my thirty years in journalism, I have witnessed, pardon the pun, the decline of our justice system, and it must stop. We need reform from top to bottom. We need transparency, where folks can actually see the corrupt judges and greedy lawyers, actually witness their fellow citizens being legally blackmailed or railroaded.

One of my favorite parts of Wendy Murphy's book is her anger at the so-called restorative justice concept, which has taken root in Vermont and Minnesota. I call this "wind-chime" jurisprudence. The basic premise is that for a crime to be fully adjudicated, everyone involved must be "healed." Of course, that includes the criminal who is not to be severely punished for his violation, but rehabilitated so that he realizes he must be much nicer in the future. Somewhere very warm, Al Capone is grinning.

Restorative justice, the promulgation of unscrupulous tactics, lying to the media, and other modern legal techniques, are all analyzed and scorched by Wendy Murphy, who uses her pen like a blowtorch. If only the legal system had Wendy's passion and compassion. If only the mercenary lawyers, corrupt judges, a deceitful press, and all the others who have made the courthouse a dangerous place, would adopt a sense of fairness and a knowledge of right and wrong.

The first step toward any reform is an exposition of the corruption. This book does that about as well as it can be done. It gets under the legal mumbo jumbo and offers you, the reader, strategies to avoid getting your head kicked in if, God forbid, you wind up in a courtroom. It also offers a challenge to the powerful in America: Reform our legal system or admit it's a farce.

In her remarkable career as an attorney and child advocate, Wendy Murphy has accomplished much, including chasing numerous bad guys down and holding them accountable. She has comforted the afflicted and annoyed the oppressors. She has stood for good and challenged evil in a way that is both vivid and effective.

However, in my opinion, *And Justice for Some* is her towering achievement. I am honored to be able to introduce it to you.

Bill O'Reilly
Long Island, New York
February 11, 2007

Contents

Contents

Contents

AND JUSTICE FOR SOME

INTRODUCTION

You Call This Justice?

LET'S OPEN WITH A TRUE HORROR STORY.

A man in Vermont named Mark Hulett raped a little girl countless times over a four-year period, beginning when she was seven years old. In 2005, he was caught, tried, and convicted of the hideous crimes, to which he ultimately confessed. The prosecutor sought a sentence of eight to ten years.

The judge in the case, Edward Cashman, sentenced the rapist to just sixty days in prison.

Explaining his decision to the astonished courtroom, Judge Cashman said that when he first was elevated to the bench a quarter century earlier, he believed in tough sentencing. More recently, though, he had concluded that being hard-nosed with bad guys didn't serve any useful purpose. "It doesn't make anything better," he said. "It costs us a lot of money, we create a lot of expectation, and we feed on anger."

Let's stop right there, for a minute. How do you feel about that? Sixty days for inflicting four years of appalling, relentless rape and sexual abuse on a helpless child because being hard-nosed doesn't serve any useful purpose.

There's a big difference between being hard-nosed toward a criminal and coddling him like a child who's stolen a pack of gum. What's the obvious message to all the child molesters lurking out there? How about the monster who lives in your neighborhood?

When Fox News's Bill O'Reilly ran a clip of Cashman on his show, O'Reilly told his audience: "You may be looking at the worst judge in the U.S.A."

I agree that Cashman's in the running—although he has lots of competition for the title. And guess what: It's not only the judges we have to worry about. There's a whole slew of defense attorneys out there who are equally willing—probably even more willing—to put *you* at risk of harm by dishonoring the justice system as well as the right of all law-abiding citizens to live in a world where dangerous criminals aren't allowed to run around free in society.

Do I sound angry? I am. And I want you to get angry, too.

Back when I was in law school, not all that many years ago, it was common to hear some version of the following: We Americans have the best legal system in the world.

We don't hear this very much anymore. You know why?

Because we don't have the best legal system in the world. We have the best system if you're a criminal. We actually have an awful system if you're a victim or a law-abiding citizen.

I wrote this book because I think we can do better. I've read enough of the Constitution to know that it wasn't designed to produce such unfairness. In the wake of the terrorist attacks of 9/11, we've all been paying a little more attention to the words written by the founders of our country. With a revived common fear and concern for the well-being of all Americans, we have come together as a nation in a way that has breathed new life into fundamental American values. I hope we keep it up—especially on the most basic of principles—such as the one that is spelled out in simple yet poignant terms at the end of our pledge to one another; a pledge we make as equal investors in a nation unafraid to fight, even die, for common beliefs that unite us despite the vast array of differences that distinguish us from one another. ". . . with liberty and justice for all." Let me repeat that last part *for all*—not just some.

Today, this pledge is being dishonored by the people who run our justice system. We know this because we can see the unbelievable shenanigans as criminals get away with murder, while the rest of us—if I can speak for the rest of us—get indigestion watching one smug thug after another walk away from his crimes scot-free. I bet you can conjure up such an image: a man who should be in prison boasting about his victory on the courthouse steps, crowing into the microphones and TV cameras with a smirking lawyer by his side.

This book is full of attacks on defense attorneys but let me be clear—lots of attorneys who represent disgusting human

3

beings play by the rules and never go over the line. These are the lawyers who deserve our utmost respect—and there are plenty of them out there. One of my dearest friends, Arthur Kelly, represented one of the men who raped and killed a little boy named Jeffrey Curley. Arthur fought hard to make sure the guy got a fair trial and although the defendant was convicted, Arthur suffered terrible public scorn for doing his job well. That's not fair because even though he represented a despicable human being, he played by the rules, which is more than I can say about most of the defense attorneys I criticize in this book. My beef is with the lawyers who cheat to win. Cheating has nothing to do with justice.

Criminal justice was supposed to mean prosecuting a criminal in a just way. Instead, today, it means letting a criminal lie, cheat, and manipulate his way out of trouble—or coddling a criminal at the expense of an innocent victim. Sure, we should have compassion for some of the people behind bars. Some of them have good hearts and wound up in a dire situation due to a combination of tough luck and very bad judgment. Sure, we should cut a guy some slack if, at the end of the day, he has the potential to care about others.

But an awful lot of people who commit crimes don't give a damn about anyone else. Maybe it's because they were abused, or maybe just because nobody ever cared about them. (This happens more often than we'd like to think.) In some situations, a terrible thing happened that made them hate the world, and the rest of us have to pay the consequences when crime occurs.

Some people think it doesn't matter why bad guys do what they do. I disagree. I believe that if we could do a better job intervening in the lives of troubled kids before they became law-breaking adults, there would be far less crime in general, kids would stand a better chance at becoming successful adults, and we'd save a ton of money, to boot. But in fact, we've never dedicated enough resources to crime prevention, mainly because as a society we're hopelessly shortsighted. We don't really think much about crime until it happens to us, or to someone we love—or until the media serve up a wayward celebrity for our entertainment.

But the fact that we don't devote enough resources to prevention is no excuse for going soft on criminals when they do get caught. In today's society, we live at close quarters. We have to interact without hurting one another. Tough punishment for criminals is a powerful reminder that we are all under contract to treat each other with civility. This contract—unwritten yet the critical underpinning of our society—says that each of us has both rights *and* responsibilities—not just rights!

Let me say that a little more bluntly. Too many people in this country think the criminal law is designed *only* to protect and enforce the rights of the bad guys. This is simply not true. The Constitution expressly mandates an ordered liberty—not some sort of criminal chaos. Our founding fathers clearly intended that while we enjoyed our hard-won freedoms, we would also exercise our constitutional duty to be civilized to one another.

Unfortunately, our criminal justice system sends exactly the opposite message. All too often, it gives criminals a pass on the responsibilities part—a get-out-of-jail-free card, if you will—while overemphasizing the rights part of the citizenship bargain.

I first got exposed to this corrupt reality as a young prosecutor. I came to my job as an idealist, but that didn't last long. In case after case, the message that I saw conveyed to the criminal was: Now that you've been caught, the system will kiss your butt. True, you may go to prison if you're convicted, which, by the way, is not very likely in the majority of criminal prosecutions. But even if you're among the unlucky few who do wind up in jail, you will almost never get the time you deserve, and you may well get out ahead of schedule.

Meanwhile, between the time you're arrested for your crime and the day the judge finally sentences you, the system will bend over backward not only to be fair—which I believe to be a good thing—but also to make you comfortable and make your victim miserable, which I believe to be a bad thing.

And if you're prosecuted in a state like Massachusetts, where I practice, you can engage in all kinds of malicious mischief. What do I mean by mischief? Get this. Once you're charged with a crime, you are actually permitted to do harmful things to your victims. For example, you can use taxpayer dollars to hire a private investigator to harass your victim's family and friends. You can use the authority of the government's subpoena powers to conduct fishing expeditions in your victim's private medical files. And in virtually every state in the union—not just liberal Massachusetts—if you're a criminal, you can literally commit perjury with impunity by testifying falsely under oath.

This is seriously embarrassing and frustrating and dangerous. President Clinton was nearly thrown out of office for lying about a noncriminal sexual event, but murderers and rapists commit perjury every day in courtrooms across this country, and the justice system does absolutely nothing about it. These are things that a citizen who hasn't committed a crime can't get away with.

One more time: If you don't commit a crime, you can't spend public dollars harassing crime victims and witnesses, and you can't lie under oath and get away with it. But if you rape someone or beat someone to death and then you get caught, you can.

This insanity is going on every day all across this country, and nobody is doing anything about it. In fact, to the contrary, victims are being told that the system is tough, and the trial will be brutal. In the face of all this, how can we possibly expect people to report crimes and testify in criminal cases? If crimes aren't reported and citizens don't testify, how can the government ensure the public's safety?

It's a truly unbelievable situation. Victims and witnesses to crime who cooperate with the justice system deserve good-citizenship awards. Instead, they get a kick in the head, and we tell them tough luck, in so many words.

Wasn't our pledge to one another a promise of *justice for all*? Isn't justice supposed to be about truth and fairness? So how is it that time and time again we see nothing but lies and trickery? Justice for some? Maybe. Justice for *all*? Not a chance.

After twenty years in this system, I can tell you that things have grown increasingly out of control. I see judges who give child–sex offenders probation. I see defense attorneys who lie through their teeth, and victims and witnesses who succumb to outright corruption. I even see victim advocates showing up on the defense side of things. I'm not kidding. The Vermont

Coalition Against Sexual Assault said essentially nothing to criticize Judge Cashman for sentencing a brutal child rapist to only sixty days in prison. They said instead that mandatory punishments are not necessarily appropriate for dangerous sex offenders.

As if that weren't bad enough, the Massachusetts Office on Victims' Assistance (MOVA)—the organization that is supposed to fight hard to *protect* victims' rights—actually proposed legislation in 2004 to *take away* victims' rights. Let me explain. A hard-fought case gave victims the right to directly address the court to seek enforcement of their speedy trial rights, but rather than celebrating the victory, MOVA responded by proposing a new law that had the effect of undermining the ruling. This new law would have required victims to first obtain permission from the prosecutor *before* addressing the court. And it would have limited what victims could say to the judge about violations of their speedy trial rights. After victim advocates around the country brought pressure to bear on legislative sponsors of the bill, the proposal was withdrawn, but people continue to raise eyebrows about MOVA's motivation in proposing a new law to hurt victims' rights.

Maybe we shouldn't be surprised that some victims' groups care more about criminals' rights than victims' rights. After all, the National Organization for Women was nowhere to be found when the victim in the Kobe Bryant case was getting her proverbial butt kicked all over the planet. After much criticism for their silence, NOW issued such a limp statement that it would have been better if they'd continued to say nothing.

I find this especially galling because when I give lectures all over the country on sexual violence, I see the same poster of NOW's president calling for an end to "the silencing" of rape victims. Are you scratching your head yet? Victims should be brave and break the silence, but NOW stays mute when they need support. That's effective, don't you think?

The National Organization for Women was only too happy to condemn Senator Bob Packwood in 1995 for sexually harassing women in his office, but NOW was essentially silent when President Clinton was being serviced by Monica Lewinsky under his desk in the Oval Office, even after other women credibly accused him of even more serious misconduct. What's going on here? How can groups that claim to care about violence against women go silent in certain cases and scream from the rooftops about the very same type of harm in other cases? I'm not sure I know the answer, but I'm certain that this hypocrisy is why so little is being accomplished in the fight against violence against women. NOW has to stop pretending to speak for all "women's issues" and allow the development of true leadership to emerge. Men and women should be working together in the fight against violence against women. But to win the fight, they need to transcend the stranglehold of partisan obedience.

The failure of antiviolence activism is likely the result of a leftover classical liberal ideology that invigorated the women's movement in the 1970s but served to co-opt and silence women who were fighting for better laws to prevent rape. Simply put, liberal elites managed to persuade lots of women's advocates that the rights of criminals are more important than the right of innocent people to be protected from sexual violence. I just don't get this mind-set. Sure I want strong protections for people accused of crime. Liberty for all of us is compromised when criminals don't receive due process. But liberty also suffers when whole classes of innocent people, like women and children, feel terrorized just going about their lives as law-abiding citizens. It's unreasonable for people who claim to be victims' advocates to put criminals' rights at the top of their list of priorities.

Many groups are starting to change, but it's tough because victims' groups get more money and accolades when they either stand up for criminals or stay silent. There isn't a lot of ideologically-based political support and applause when groups criticize the legal system as "too lenient" on the perpetrator. I see a lot of hope, though, because I get "anonymous" calls from advocates who ask for advice about how to make their organization fight harder for victims. And although I get marginalized by some advocates who think that because I'm tough on criminals, I'm somehow unqualified to sit with them and ask the tough questions about how they're spending their time and resources, growing numbers of advocates are fighting for real reforms to help protect innocent people from devastating harm.

People tell me I sound "fascist," "conservative," "liberal," "radical," and even "communist." The only thing nobody calls me is a capitalist and the funny thing is that I like capitalism but it has no place in the criminal justice system. Justice should *always* be better than capitalism. But the bottom line is, all these *isms* are meaningless to me. I'm in nobody's club and this is important because no leader of a certain ilk can call me and say,

"Wendy, you need to start saying X," or "You need to stop saying Y." When it comes to antiviolence work, partisan ideologies are destructive forces that sometimes command obedience to dumb ideas.

Being an unaligned voice makes some of this work easy for me. But I'll be honest, this is painful stuff to deal with, no matter what your background. Which is why writing this book has been difficult for me, and reading it may also be tough for you. I think of those jurors who acquitted an obviously guilty child–rapist because they just couldn't believe that someone could commit a horrible act of violence against an adorable three-year-old little girl. In that same spirit of willful ignorance, some people who read this book may not be able to face the truth. The truth will be too scary and too frightening.

Like you, I prefer to think of the world as safe. I'm the mother of five young kids. Frankly, it feels a whole lot better to assume the world is not a dangerous place when I send my children off to school every morning. But the sad reality is that crime happens all the time—and we are all at risk. Sexual violence, in particular, occurs with astounding frequency. In fact, it's hard to find an adult who hasn't been sexually assaulted at some point in his or her life. Ask around. Listen hard, and read between the lines. Don't be surprised by the answers. Measuring incidence rates is difficult because so few sex crimes are reported to police but some studies show that one in four females and one in six males is victimized by a completed or attempted sex crime. In the book *The Epidemic of Rape and Child Sexual Abuse in the United States* (Thousand Oaks, CA: Sage Publications, 2000), Diana Russell and Rebecca Bolen write that 38 percent of girls under age eighteen are victimized by sexual abuse. Experts estimate that costs attributable to sexual violence amount to over $1.2 billion a year. It's time to get outraged!

This book is full of stories that will make you feel angry, sad, shocked, and perhaps even terrified. Please don't turn away. The truth is too important: The very justice system that claims to be keeping us safe is in fact giving away the store to criminals and beating the figurative hell out of innocent victims. And the worst part is the judges and lawyers whom we count on to serve as guardians of the system—the so-called officers of the court— are responsible for most of the trouble.

I tried fighting for change as a prosecutor. But after one too many judges told me that my job was to "state the law, not complain about it," I gave up. I became a lawyer for victims in the real world.

I had two kids by the time I decided to leave the prosecutor's office. This personal reality made my professional decision much easier. As a young mother, I'd grown tired of telling other parents the shocking truth: that the system cared much more about rapists than rape victims. Day after day, the cases came at me, and the staggering number of children being brutalized was tearing my heart out. It was getting hard to go home every night and see my toddlers' trusting faces. Was spending all my time trying to put people behind bars for hurting kids the right thing for me to be doing? Was I actually helping to protect my own family? The reporting of child abuse and sex crimes seemed at epidemic proportions. Could my children possibly be safe?

I was lucky enough to have excellent day care. My aunt

cared for my children at her home and she could not have been more loving and protective. But in the pile of cases on my desk, I could see that parents just like me were discovering every day that their kids had been hurt by someone they trusted—someone they believed was a loving caregiver.

One day, I asked my two-year-old son what he had done that day at Auntie's. In his loud but imprecise little voice, he replied, "I eat Tom's penis." If you're a parent, you know exactly how I felt. I nearly passed out. After composing myself, I started asking questions. "What room were you in?" "Was Auntie there?" "What was Tom doing?" When I asked this last question, my son replied, "He pick up da shells on da floor." I started laughing. My precious little boy had been eating Tom's peanuts. Tom had been picking up the shells. All was well! But during that endless split second, when I was thinking that the worst of the world had intruded on my own family and that a criminal case might be at hand, I realized something terrible. I realized that I—as someone who understood the system and could make sure it was as fair as possible—would not allow my own child to endure the suffering that would surely come with participation in a criminal trial.

This meant, in turn, that absolutely nothing would be done in my child's (imaginary) case. Which made me realize that it was time to stop killing myself inside a badly broken system, where the criminals were laughing and the good guys were crying. As a prosecutor, there was little I could do to make things better. But if I left the district attorney's office, I concluded, I could really make a difference.

Fifteen years later, I'm writing this book, in part, because I have made a difference. I've had real success—satisfying, gratifying success—fighting for victims, and I want to share my strategies with you so that you can help, too.

But before you can get involved, you have to understand how the system works, and why things are broken so badly. It's essential for you to learn as much as you can about the challenges before us so that you can participate effectively in public discussions about criminal-justice matters and so that you can become a great advocate for a better legal system.

This book will give you insight into why terrible things happen to innocent people all the time. And it will help you fight back by letting you in on some of the dirty tricks and evil tactics that undermine the integrity of our justice system. Read it and weep, but don't stop there.

Do something about it!

ONE

Murphy's Law, Rewritten

You've heard of Murphy's Law. It's the one that says, "if something can go wrong, it will go wrong, at the worst possible moment."

I propose to rewrite Murphy's Law. From now on, I want (Wendy) Murphy's Law to read, "It can't go wrong if people like you and me don't let it."

Before you can buy that rewrite, though, you need to know a little more about me.

In the past two decades, I've been a prosecutor, a law professor at the New England School of Law, a lecturer at the Massachusetts Institute of Technology, a Visiting Scholar at Harvard

Law School, and a legal analyst for CBS News, MSNBC, and CNN.

For what it's worth, I've appeared as a pundit—a certified voice of authority—on virtually every major network and cable news show. I've also served as an editor and writer for a national antiviolence publication.

As a prosecutor in Massachusetts, I handled literally hundreds of cases. As an attorney in private practice, I've sued powerful institutions, generated many appellate decisions through impact litigation, and published countless academic and pop culture articles.

I've worked with Congress and state legislatures to change laws. I've written dozens of briefs for appellate courts around the nation. I've consulted on cases impacting the lives of women and children around the world. I even took on Harvard and made them change their rules to be fairer to victims of sex crimes on campus, and I beat the military when they tried to force a rape victim's counselor to turn over her file in a court-martial rape case.

I've served on numerous boards and commissions, given many speeches to thousands of people across the country, and worked my butt off representing crime victims for free.

In between, I gave birth to five children. Four of them came to court with me within days of their birth, with my youngest making her debut at the Massachusetts Supreme Judicial Court at the ripe old age of two-and-a-half days.

What else? I have a closet full of awards. I've been named Activist Mother of the Year by *Glamour* magazine, and celebrated as Lawyer of the Year in Massachusetts. I received an award from the National Sexual Violence Resource Center and was honored with the first-ever prize for outstanding advocacy for crime victims from the National Crime Victim Law Institute—not only for developing new concepts and practices but also for pushing the justice system relentlessly to make it work better for the good guys.

I'm not telling you all this to boast. I could write just as lengthy a book about the things I've done wrong in my career.

I'm giving you all this background about me because I want you to understand that I speak from experience. I also want you to realize that you, one single person, can make a big difference if you feel strongly enough about a cause. People who work tirelessly for victims need to support each other and talk to lots of people, proudly, about what they do. Too many people who work hard in this fight every single day toil in isolation and never get the pat on the back they deserve. Most prosecutors, for example, regularly put in more than a full work week making sure laws are enforced, but they get little of what I call "cultural self-esteem"—the feeling that what they do, for very little pay, is appreciated by the public. I want that to change. And I want to get more of you involved in making things better. So this book is designed to help you appreciate that this is very difficult but also very rewarding work.

People who fight for victims need more support from people like you. Why? Because unlike the fight for criminals' rights, this work is not part of the political machine. There's no big clanking infrastructure behind it, supported by influential dialogues or even taxpayer dollars and special interest groups. Also, it's a tough job to do psychologically. Dealing with unimaginable horrors every day makes it nearly impossible to go home and act like a "normal" human being. You either become jaded and cynical or paranoid about the dangers lurking just around the corner in your personal life. I struggle, but I still keep at it, mainly because I believe I have a responsibility, as an attorney, to better promote the true meaning and integrity of the word "justice."

But it's not easy. So when you come across someone doing this kind of work, thank him or her. If you are already helping out, thank you. And if you meet someone doing harm to the system, don't hesitate to let them know how you feel even if it means criticizing an attorney.

It used to infuriate me to hear mean-spirited jokes about attorneys, but not anymore! I've grown disgusted with too many of my colleagues—the lawyers and lawyers-turned-judges who bring shame to my profession by lying, cheating, and manipulating the system to cause unjust results.

Contrary to the sort of nonsense we heard from countless defense attorneys after the O. J. Simpson debacle, when dirty tricks hurt victims or allow the most dangerous of criminals to walk around free in society, it's absolutely not *good for liberty*. Simpson's acquittal was not something to be proud of; it was revolting. Yet people in my profession actually cheered when they learned of the "not guilty" verdict, as they often do when a guilty criminal wins, no matter how it happened. When a vicious murderer dupes a jury into voting not guilty because his lawyers found an expert willing to testify (for a price) that "Twinkies made him do it," defense attorneys actually high-five each other—as if undercutting the system were something to celebrate.

To make matters worse, most ex-prosecutors become defense attorneys; and when they switch sides, they no longer have an incentive to fight the injustices and dirty tricks. In fact, they start using the dirty tricks themselves in order to win cases. I could easily have become a defense attorney, but I stayed on the victims' side of things when I left the prosecutor's office because I knew it was important to have a former insider working on behalf of victims and speaking openly about the scandalous problems that plague our justice system.

Defense attorneys routinely get media coverage for their complaints about the system from the perspective of the criminal. But how much is ever said about the ways our legal system causes harm to victims and law-abiding citizens? How many of you are even aware of a recent study that found that one in five of you will become a crime victim and nearly half of those victimized won't even report the crime to the police? Theories abound about why this is so, but what I hear every day is that people don't believe in the system anymore. The feeling is: Why bother reporting a crime? The justice process is slow, painful, and usually results in the wrong verdict or such little punishment that it's not worth the time or trouble. Criminals don't feel this way—victims and law-abiding citizens do. Criminals are having a field day lodging complaints about everything under the sun and insisting on broad-based reforms.

For example, the fact that a public defender fell asleep in court—one day many years ago—made front-page headlines and incited calls for large-scale changes to the benefit of accused criminals. But how often does it make the news, or provoke a protest, when an accused criminal intimidates a victim or his lawyer pulls a dirty trick? Answer: almost never.

This is important not only because how we administer justice matters but also because the public has a right to know how and when their money is being wasted. Our court system is paid for by tax dollars, which means everything that happens is, to some extent, controlled by us. We have a right to know how every dollar is spent, especially if the system is causing harm to innocent people who are doing nothing more than complying with their civic duty to testify in criminal court.

Today, nearly all criminals have access to lawyers, many paid for by us, the taxpayers. And one of the best-kept secrets is that lots of criminals aren't really poor but lie about their situation or hide their assets so that we have to foot the bill for their defense. Soon after pedophile priest John Geoghan became the focus of a criminal investigation in Massachusetts for sexually abusing little boys, he transferred his interest in two properties—one was an ocean-front estate—to his sister for one dollar. By the time he needed an attorney to represent him at trial, he claimed to be indigent. This got him a lawyer paid for by the public. He should have been forced to rescind his fraudulent transfer of wealth and at least pay something for an attorney. But instead, we, the taxpayers, paid; and apparently nobody gave a damn about the colossal waste of the public's money, or the fact that an accused child molester was perpetrating a heinous fraud. Geoghan virtually stole money away from truly poor defendants who legitimately needed publicly-funded lawyers to protect their rights.

If there were better oversight of public defenders' budgets, fraud could be prevented and more money would be available for all sorts of things to help the system work better. Think about this. What if some of the money could be used to pay for victims to have lawyers? Obviously this would help, because, remember, the prosecutor does not represent the victim. A criminal prosecution is not a private lawsuit. The government brings the charges against the defendant. The victim is merely a witness for the prosecution and, unlike accused criminals, witnesses have no right to legal counsel. This does not mean a victim can't go out and hire her own lawyer. Some do, and I've been representing victims in criminal cases, for free, for fifteen years. But a victim cannot claim a constitutional *right* to an attorney, and most cannot afford to hire one.

If more public funds were available, judges might be more willing to appoint lawyers to help indigent victims, but budgets are tight and defense opposition to victims having private lawyers is fierce. So even with careful oversight of spending, we're not likely to see a comprehensive victim-attorney program any time soon. Still, if spending were reined in a bit and public defenders' budgets were regularly scrutinized for waste and misuse of funds, the money saved could at least be redirected away from supporting dirty tricks and harmful tactics. This alone would give victims a better shot at justice.

There are some government funds available for lawyers who do what I call victim hand-holding. These lawyers go to court with victims and sit with them while they get whacked around. Other victim lawyers provide civil legal services, such as helping a victim with housing problems and assisting a battered woman in obtaining a protective order. While we need more public money for all kinds of victim services, restrictions limit the ways public dollars can be spent, and some of these rules literally prohibit lawyers to challenge roadblocks to justice within the criminal justice system—which, of course, is where most of the shenanigans are going on.

What we really need is private funding for unaffiliated victim lawyers.

We need lots and lots of private money to fund *nonprofit* lawyers and law firms so that victim attorneys can fight for the rights of the innocent while defense lawyers fight for the rights of the guilty. I'm not saying that all victims' rights are equal in weight to all defendants' rights—just that there should be someone whose job it is to argue zealously on behalf of the victim. The prosecutor can't do it because he or she represents the state, and the state represents the people—which sounds promising enough but is, in fact, a double-edged sword. The prosecutor actually has a responsibility to protect the rights of the accused, even while he or she is trying to convict that individual. If you're a victim, in other words, the prosecutor isn't really on *your* side; he or she is actually on everybody's side.

I don't have a problem with the limits on prosecutors, but what they do is far from real advocacy for the *personal* rights of victims. In fact, due to the restrictions of professional ethics rules, prosecutors aren't even allowed to represent victims in a personal capacity. Again, privately funded, independent attorneys are needed to fill this void.

Family Justice Centers are a recent innovation intended to address a piece of the problem, at least to some extent. They're designed to help victims feel more comfortable reporting crimes and subsequently stay involved in the criminal justice system. These centers are a good start because they offer victims "one-stop shopping" when a crime occurs. The victim goes to the center and gets access to all relevant law enforcement and community–based service providers under one roof. Again, this approach helps victims stay connected to the system, which in turn increases the likelihood that justice will be served.

There are a few problems, however.

First, these centers exist in only a few states.

Second, for a variety of reasons, their impact most likely will be limited to family and interpersonal violence.

Third, Family Justice Centers receive federal funds, which means even if they existed in every state, victims would still need independent legal advocacy in the criminal courtroom—lawyers who can stand up in court, without ethical or public-funding restraints, and advocate aggressively just for the victim.

In addition to private attorneys, victims need more opportunities to speak out publicly when injustice happens. Let's face it: We live in a media world. When it comes to holding the system accountable, there's nothing as effective as a powerful TV appearance by a victim, or a victim's advocate. Everyone on television has at least a little ego involved; but, for some of us, we're also on television because of our strong convictions that punditry is an indispensable part of the recipe for change. Maybe you saw me screaming at a defense attorney on CBS's *The Early Show* for saying, in so many words: The fact that Michael Jackson sleeps with little boys doesn't mean he's a pedophile. Did he say that with a straight face?

Or maybe you've caught me on the *O'Reilly Factor*, criticizing a judge or a prosecutor for agreeing to probation for a child rapist. This is important work, and I'm glad to be able to speak up for victims on television. We all have to speak up in whatever venues we have because we are all part of public oversight, and together we can provide immeasurable benefits to the integrity of the system simply by taking the time to notice and to say something when injustice happens.

I'm certainly not suggesting that judges' decisions should be guided primarily by opinion polls. An independent judiciary is important and public opinion sometimes goes wrong. But it is essential that the public's perspective be brought to bear on the definition of "justice" because it is a core concept around which society is organized. Judges and prosecutors are supposed to take the victim's and the public's opinion into account when they make decisions in the name of justice. But too often these viewpoints are ignored, simply because the people in charge assume that nobody is watching.

We have to show them that we are watching.

Media celebrities like Bill O'Reilly and agitators like me may not effect changes in the law in quite the same way as when a brilliant brief is filed in court. But the truth is that sometimes standing up for victims on television has a huge impact because there's no defense attorney or judge complaining that victims and their lawyers have "no right to be heard." This is a common reaction to the idea that victims should have lawyers in criminal cases. I ignore this, of course, though I understand the sentiment. When I was a prosecutor it made me nervous when a victim showed up with a lawyer, but things are so out of control now, with defendants being allowed unprecedented authority to intrude in the private lives of victims, the system has no choice but to allow victims to be represented by private lawyers. This could be avoided if defendants and their lawyers were restricted to dealing *only* with the prosecution and were prohibited from intruding into the private lives of victims and witnesses. But so long as these impositions are allowed, victims must be entitled to assert all their rights with the assistance of private attorneys. I routinely appear in court for victims and when someone says my client has no right to heard, I cite the Constitution and any other law I can find that arguably authorizes me to be there fighting for a person who has suffered enough and wants nothing more than for justice to be served.

This book is a call to arms. It is a shout-out to you and to all those who think the way we do justice matters—even if you never step one foot inside a courtroom. Why do I inject myself into criminal cases on behalf of victims? Because I want the world I live in to be a place that cares about fairness, and I want the people who suffer to have a voice. I believe that anyone who wants a *just* legal system has an obligation to do something about the horrible system we have now. It's important to teach our kids about fairness and the importance of treating others with respect. But if we really want children to grow up in a world where mutual respect is the first order of business, we have to hold our legal system accountable when chaos, corruption, and sneaky tricks control the courthouse because mutual respect is not possible when the rule of law itself is unjust.

No, it isn't easy. I've often told people that for me, fighting against injustice is like climbing a mountain of ice while wearing plastic slippers. It's cold, I don't get much traction, and the surface is solid and relentlessly unforgiving. But I keep on climbing because that's what it takes to tackle such a big problem. I'm sure other people in my position have similar stories to tell, and it is important for us to work together and share stories—to get the word out about what's really going on. The more of us who tackle the mountain, in one way or another, the faster we will see the benefits of an improved justice system—like safer streets, fewer school shootings, less online sexual exploitation of children, longer prison sentences, treatment for all criminals during incarceration, more judicial accountability, and—ultimately—less crime.

At the beginning of the chapter, I proposed a rewrite of Murphy's Law to get us out of a defeatist mind-set and on track for success. Now that we've covered some of the basics, it's time for the tough stuff. We can't stop things from going wrong without getting a handle on the dirty tricks that provide the foundation for much of what's wrong in our courtrooms. They often go unnoticed, and people like you rarely complain, because you haven't yet been let in on the secrets.

Let the unveiling begin.

Two

Manufacturing Innocence with DNA Lies

LET'S GET ONE THING ON THE TABLE RIGHT AWAY. There's nothing wrong with zealous advocacy for accused criminals. Public relations people are paid to spin, and lawyers are paid to advocate. The more energetically you do it, assuming you have the necessary smarts and skills, the more effective you're going to be—usually.

Zealous advocacy is what great lawyers do. It's perfectly fair to try and persuade a judge or jury or the public to see things in a certain light—in fact, it's your job. But lying about evidence is not spin or advocacy, it's fraud. One of the biggest frauds being perpetrated in the criminal justice system today is the claim that nearly two hundred convicted criminals have been declared innocent as a result of new DNA tests that have been conducted on old cases. The truth is that most of the criminals whose convictions have been overturned because of DNA tests actually have not been proved innocent. Read those stories, and listen to news reports carefully. The word that they use is "exonerated." What the stories don't tell you is that a person can be legally "exonerated" and one hundred percent factually "guilty." This means that some of the stories are at best misleading, and at worst false.

No, this is not a criticism of all, or even many, defense attorneys. The vast majority of lawyers who defend criminals are honest people, sincere in their advocacy for clients they don't even like. It makes me proud of my profession that lawyers are willing to represent dangerous and evil people because it takes a lot of courage, discipline, and commitment to the core values of a free society to stand next to a monster and insist that he deserves to be set free—even if guilty—because the government didn't prove its case. This is a noble thing to do, period. I won't even add any qualifications about how the worst thugs shouldn't get the best possible representation. Thugs deserve due process; and defense attorneys deserve a lot of credit for making sure we adhere to this important principle.

Defense attorneys deserve extra points—lots of extra points—for being the heroes of the truly innocent men who have been unjustly convicted. In several cases, the dogged efforts of defense counsel have led to the discovery of old evidence in dusty old files—evidence that, when submitted for DNA testing, proved scientifically that a man previously convicted of a crime was, in fact, completely innocent. It's a great story—the innocent man being released from prison and running into the waiting arms of loved ones. The media always pounce on these stories with alacrity. And in fact, it's wonderful stuff.

The problem is that we have no way of knowing how many exonerated individuals had nothing to do with the crime of which they were convicted. In a January 23, 2007, Associated Press story, a reporter cites lawyers at the Innocence Project as claiming 194 men have been exonerated through DNA tests, but there is nothing in the story about what "exonerated" means, or even a suggestion that it does not mean factually innocent. Time and time again, defense attorneys and the media claim (or falsely imply) that an individual has been proven innocent by new DNA tests. In a May 5, 2004, *Boston Herald* story on wrongful convictions, the reporter wrote that "throughout the country 143 *innocent* suspects have been freed since 1990." [My emphasis.] Misleading use of the word "exoneration" is one thing—this is an outright lie. Exoneration is a catchall word that comprises a range of possible meanings, including circumstances in which the person who is exonerated is, in fact, guilty. This is because "exonerated" can mean the guy's conviction was overturned, and he wasn't retried because the witnesses had long since died or were unavailable, or the suspect had served his whole sentence before the new DNA tests were conducted. That a conviction was overturned and a criminal not retried does *not* mean the criminal has been declared innocent. It simply means the legal system did not find him guilty. This is the same judgement reached with O. J. Simpson. Would you call him innocent?

I believe that the public has a right and a need to know the truth about which cases involve actual innocence and which cases involve a clearly guilty criminal using new DNA testing on old evidence to win a new trial. It matters a lot whether new DNA tests do nothing but muddy the waters with tangential or barely relevant evidence to help get a criminal out of jail on a technical argument about how the evidence was unavailable twenty years ago, prior to the development of DNA technology.

Defense attorneys don't mind if the word "exonerated" is misunderstood to mean actual innocence. In fact, they benefit from the confusion. Lots of them have been gaining political power—and winning boatloads of money—by suing the government on behalf of exonerated men. Clearly this business venture would be far less lucrative if the distinction weren't so blurry. Why? Because representing a guilty man who was properly convicted but just happened to get off—not because he's innocent, or even because the government did something wrong, but because DNA science wasn't around at the time of his trial—doesn't make for much of a lawsuit on the face of it. But representing a factually innocent man who was wrongfully imprisoned can be worth a hell of a lot of money in a lawsuit. It's no wonder that clever lawyers try to make the former situation look like the latter one with murky terminology like "exonerated."

Lots of public dollars are wasted settling lawsuits filed against the government on behalf of exonerated-but-factually-guilty men, and nobody seems to care. Our tax money is being delivered in ribbon-wrapped wheelbarrows to murderers and rapists who deserved to be punished, to apologize to them even though the trial was fair, because of something that nobody could have prevented.

Shouldn't we at least be keeping track of how public money is being spent in these cases? Shouldn't someone be checking to see whether government officials are paying excessive and quick settlements not because a completely innocent man spent half his life in prison—which is a very rare occurrence that deserves compensation—but because it's the politically expedient thing to do?

The media bear some of the blame for this fiasco because it is difficult to find a reporter who is willing to write about the difference between exonerated and innocent. Conversely, it's all too easy to find people willing to parrot false but oft-repeated misleading claims like "more than 150 innocent men have been cleared through new DNA tests." Exonerated, yes; innocent, no.

But it gets worse. Certain reporters seem only too eager to challenge facts that work against the interests of the guilty. Take the simple fact that sex offenders have a disproportionately high recidivism rate. ("Recidivism" simply means committing additional offenses after the first one.) Benjamin Radford, a reporter for a bimonthly magazine called the *Skeptical Enquirer*—wrote in 2006 that assertions of high recidivism were false and little more than fear-mongering. Sex offenders, Radford argued, have a lower recidivism rate than other criminals. To support his position, he cited federal data showing that "just 5 percent" of convicted sex offenders were rearrested for a sex crime in the three-year period after their release from prison. He argued that this meant that sex offenders are no more likely to reoffend than other types of criminals. "There seems little justification for the public's fear," he concluded.

But Radford conveniently neglected to mention that the federal data he cited looked only at rearrest rates—not reoffense rates. Given that 90 percent of child–sex crimes are never reported, much less lead to arrest, it hardly makes sense to declare anything about recidivism based on the numbers of times these perpetrators are rearrested. Radford also ignored research that emphasizes the importance of measuring recidivism by looking at long-term data. In fact, three years is a woefully inadequate time period in which to learn the truth about reoffense patterns for any particular sex offender. Here's the hard truth: Sex offenders are so damn sneaky and so manipulative in causing their victims not to report the crime that they are almost never caught, much less arrested or prosecuted within three years. It is this extra fog of evil—rather than exemplary behavior upon their release from prison—that explains the low recidivism rate in the federal study cited by Radford.

This isn't just my opinion; lots of research backs me up. When researchers study recidivism by asking offenders about their behavior, rather than by looking at arrest rates, the numbers are shocking—in fact, unbelievably so. In research documented by Dr. Anna Salter in her book *Predators*, when offenders were told they had to tell the truth in order to be released on parole, they revealed having molested, on average, about a dozen victims each. When they were told they would be subjected to a polygraph examination to test their honesty, many changed their answers—and reported, on average, nearly seventy victims each. And according to a study funded by the National Institutes of Mental Health, the average child molester abuses 117 victims over the course of their lifetime.

I wish Radford's poor reporting were an unusual case, but it isn't. The media spend far more energy writing about offenders' rights, while simultaneously turning a blind eye to the truth about the men exonerated by new DNA tests. We all need to read these kinds of stories with a more critical eye and an appropriate level of skepticism.

I'm not saying that we should doubt the power of DNA science to establish conclusively the identity of a person whose blood or other body fluid is found at a crime scene. We shouldn't. But the important things to remember are that

1) finding a particular person's DNA does not necessarily mean that he committed the crime
2) not finding a particular person's DNA doesn't necessarily mean that he didn't.

One notorious example is the 1989 Central Park Jogger case, in which a young woman was brutally attacked in New York's Central Park and left for dead. Many young men committed this ghastly crime together, and five were convicted after confessions to the crime in detail and on videotape, four in the presence of adult relatives. Only one of them, a man named Matias Reyes, left DNA on the victim's body. Did the absence of DNA from the other offenders mean that they committed no crime? No, it only meant they didn't leave any strong biological evidence at the scene. And it matters not one whit that DNA technology was not available in 1989 or that the guy whose

DNA they did find, Reyes, claimed in 2002 to have acted alone. That guy, a convicted criminal, in prison for a long stretch, could have a dozen reasons he might take the heat for the others. It really doesn't matter. What counts are the confessions of the five young men whose DNA was not found at the scene—confessions that were videotaped and in almost every case taken in the presence of the suspect's parent—were credible enough to establish guilt beyond a reasonable doubt. The judge eventually threw out the five convictions in 2002 after Reyes came forward, but as I said before: DNA and the absence of DNA does not necessarily tell the whole story.

Take another example, this one hypothetical, in which a drug addict who is indebted to his dealer agrees to kidnap and deliver a child to that dealer for sexual services as payment. Most likely, only the dealer would leave DNA on or in the child's body, but both would be equally guilty of the crime. Let's say, hypothetically, that the only eyewitness to the crime saw the kidnapping but not the sexual assault. The defense would almost certainly argue—falsely—that finding the DNA of the dealer inside the child's body exonerates the kidnapper.

Now imagine that such a case took place before the development of DNA technology. This would be the kind of fact pattern an attorney for the kidnapper would use to argue for the expenditure of tax dollars so that new DNA tests could be conducted. And he would use the same argument to demand hundreds of thousands of dollars in a lawsuit against the government for his wrongful conviction, even though the absence of the kidnapper's DNA would not prove his actual innocence.

Like this hypothetical case, the majority of exonerations

involve sexual violence. In such cases, because of the nature of the crime scene (the victim's underwear or genital area) as compared to the crime scene of a murder (e.g., an entire room in a home, public park, or bar), the significance of the presence or absence of DNA is particularly likely to be overstated by defense attorneys claiming that "everything in there" is relevant.

Similarly, given that in most sex crimes cases the issue in dispute is not who committed the crime, but rather, did the defendant have the victim's consent, DNA is almost always either irrelevant or misleading on the question of guilt.

Even if the identity of the perpetrator is in dispute in a rape case, the absence of DNA in the victim's body may reveal nothing about guilt or innocence because the perpetrator may have worn a condom or failed to complete the sex act. One recent study found that 50 percent of rapes end without ejaculation. Even if no condom is used and the victim is examined immediately after the incident, it is not unusual for medical experts to find no DNA in the victim's body. In January 2007, a federal court upheld the 1999 New York conviction of Jermaine Barnes for raping a twelve-year-old child. He ejaculated and did not use a condom. The child reported the crime immediately and was taken to the hospital where a rape kit examination was performed. Not only was there no DNA found that matched Mr. Barnes's, the child's hymen was completely intact. Before you start wondering whether Mr. Barnes might be innocent, you need to know that he confessed to police in writing and on videotape. During a search of Barnes's home, police found the child's blood and Barnes's semen on a towel Mr. Barnes used to wipe himself with after the rape. Clearly, the absence of DNA is *not* proof of innocence. Likewise, the presence of someone else's DNA may reveal nothing about the perpetrator's innocence because the victim may have had consensual sex in the recent past with a partner who left his DNA at the crime scene. The fact that the crime scene is a relatively confined area, likely to contain other people's DNA for any sexually active victim, is not a reason to abandon common sense when analyzing whether the presence or absence of DNA proves an offender's actual innocence. But this is exactly what's happening in courtrooms—and by extension, in newspapers—all across the country.

Another more sinister example of when DNA can be used to distort rather than establish the truth arises when a criminal intentionally plants someone else's DNA at the crime scene—or on his own body—in order to falsely implicate an innocent person. Consider for example a recent New York case, in which murder defendant Martin Heidgen was court-ordered to open his mouth so that police could obtain a buccal (lining of the mouth) swab sample of his DNA to be compared with blood evidence found at the crime scene. The results came back "mixed," meaning that another man's DNA, as well as Heidgen's, was present. Police traced that extra DNA to a man whose semen was found inside the body of a victim from an old unsolved rape investigation.

The prosecutor said Heidgen "tried to thwart the test by mixing a sample." Defense lawyer Stephen LaMagna contended that the test had been mishandled by officials and claimed it was absurd to blame it on his client. But the judge, obviously an old pro, noted that "it would be interesting if that other sample turned out to be a wanted sex offender presently incarcerated in the [same] jail" where Heidgen was being held.

Tampering with DNA evidence would lead to widespread public outrage if a cop or a prosecutor did it. Charges would be dismissed and lawsuits would be flying in the wake of such misconduct. But what happens when a scumbag murder defendant messes with DNA evidence? Nothing. It's perfectly okay. No punishments. No lawsuits. No accountability for the harm to the system, the waste of resources, or even for falsely implicating an innocent man. Think about this. A thug can plant someone else's DNA on a piece of evidence and thereby cause a completely innocent man to be executed for a crime he did not commit—and nobody is going to do anything about it. Meanwhile, the defense attorneys in these cases are free to conduct themselves as if there's a constitutional right to cause the wrongful conviction of an innocent man.

This is an increasingly serious problem for prosecutors and police in light of popular television programs like *Law & Order* and the various *CSI* shows. Criminals learn all sorts of new tricks from the writers who have to come up with clever ideas each week to keep viewers entertained.

Memo to Hollywood: Thanks a lot.

There is room for hope, however, because one man with the power to make a difference is starting to shine an antiseptic light on this charade. Josh Marquis, the District Attorney of Clatsop County, Oregon, and the vice president of the National District Attorneys Association, explains why he has put so much of his own time and energy into exposing this fraud:

My passion has been fueled by a thirst for honesty in the debate about these important issues. It is an outright lie to call a killer or rapist "innocent" or even "exonerated" simply because a judge reversed a conviction after new DNA evidence indicated the presence of an unknown person at the crime scene, but a new trial was not possible because victims and witnesses were unable or unavailable to testify. And frankly, it cheapens the significance of those rare cases where an individual was proved factually innocent by new DNA tests. The worst part of the problem is that these fraudulent stories make people think prisons are chock full of doe-eyed innocents, and that is pure urban legend.

Marquis has written and lectured extensively on what he calls the myth of innocence. He acknowledges that holding even one innocent person on death row is unacceptable. At the same time, though, he notes that even people who are actively opposed to the death penalty—such as Judge Jed S. Rackoff of the U.S. District Court, Southern District of New York—agree that the number of innocent men who were ever on death row probably amounts to no more than thirty, despite the oft-quoted erroneous public claim that the real number is in the hundreds. This includes all cases throughout U.S. history, not just the recent spate of cases involving new DNA tests.

Marquis is guardedly optimistic that things are getting better, in terms of the public's understanding of the truth; and he points to the United States Supreme Court as proof. In its 2006 *Kansas v. Marsh* decision, the Court cited Marquis's work detailing the stories of two killers on death row, both of whom received widespread publicity in support of their claims of innocence. One of them, Ricky McGinn, even appeared on the cover of *Newsweek,* and the accompanying article hinted broadly at his probable innocence.

McGinn had been convicted in 1995 of raping and murdering his twelve-year-old stepdaughter, Stephanie Flannery, though earlier forensic tests had been unable to identify the source of a biological sample found in the child's underpants. McGinn's lawyers convinced then-Governor George W. Bush of Texas to grant McGinn a reprieve from death row so that new DNA tests could be conducted on some of the evidence found at the crime scene. In June 2000, DNA test results came back conclusively proving that McGinn had both raped and murdered the child. Did the reconfirmed truth about his guilt make the cover of *Newsweek*? You know the answer: It did not.

One thing to keep in mind is that guilty people can often persuade themselves, at least in some corner of their brain, that they're actually innocent—and that makes them very persuasive. A typical example comes from my home state of Massachusetts and involves a man named Ben LaGuer, convicted in 1984 of raping an elderly woman over an eight-hour period. LaGuer maintained his innocence and in 2002 insisted that DNA tests would set him free. After much celebratory media coverage and support from lawyers like Barry Sheck and from influential public figures like the former president of Boston University John Silber and Deval Patrick (recently elected governor of my state), new DNA tests came back proving LaGuer's guilt beyond all doubt.

LaGuer protested his innocence loudly enough to attract attention and secure the DNA tests that he wanted. The tests came back, and they conclusively reconfirmed his guilt, yet today he continues to falsely protest his innocence with intensity, and he is still filing appeals and new trial motions—at last count it was eight. Some people believe LaGuer's persistence is somehow evidence of his innocence. But consider that the same narcissistic and sociopathic tendencies that lead people to commit horrendous crimes in the first place may well propel them to relentlessly protest their innocence, even if the evidence will never clear their name. Maybe even stranger than LaGuer's persistence is the fact that lawyers, including James Rehnquist, the son of the former chief justice of the United States Supreme Court, continue to stand up for the guy. I'll always consider the unlikely possibility that a convicted criminal could be factually innocent. What I want to know is why some people find it so darn difficult to consider the far more likely reality of factual guilt despite passionate proclamations of innocence.

I don't understand why lawyers do this, except that maybe they are so blinded by some kind of anti-prosecution ideology that they don't mind spending hundreds of thousands of dollars worth of pro bono time on a case where a guy is obviously not only guilty but has had not one, not two, but eight shots at filing new trial motions and appeals. Remember murder defendant Martin Heidgen, who allegedly deposited DNA from a fellow prisoner into his own mouth so he could mess up the evidence when police took a sample from him for crime-scene testing? It appears Heidgen picked up on a trick LaGuer tried nearly twenty-five years earlier—a trick no doubt shared among countless criminals and their lawyers over the years. Like Heidgen, LaGuer was in jail awaiting trial when police got a court order to take a swab of the inside of his mouth. They wanted to conduct certain biological tests by comparing LaGuer's saliva to evidence found at the scene (they couldn't conduct DNA tests back then because it was 1983 and the technology hadn't yet been developed but they could do certain tests on saliva, which was more sensitive than blood type alone). LaGuer knew what police were planning to do, and he intentionally tampered with the sample by literally taking body fluid from a fellow prisoner and mixing it in his mouth so that when the swab was taken, police got a mixed result. Would an innocent or a guilty man try to contaminate his own saliva with the biological fluid of another person to mess up the test results? You know the answer.

Not long after the LaGuer case splashed across our papers and TV screens, CNN highlighted the case of Derek Barnabei, a man convicted in 1995 of murdering a woman named Sara Winsosky. Barnabei's supporters claimed that fingernail scrapings from the victim that had not previously been tested would prove Barnabei's innocence. In fact, tests in 2000 ultimately proved just the opposite; they proved that Barnabei was guilty. Once again, this confirmatory outcome didn't generate nearly as much news coverage as the original (false) claims of the killer's innocence.

One of the most important cases that received little truthful attention involves a man named Kerry Kotler. Kotler was one of the first and most celebrated cases of the Innocence Project. According to test results from a defense expert, Kotler was innocent of a rape for which he had previously been convicted. The Innocence Project successfully championed Kotler's release from prison in 1992 and then sued the government for his "wrongful conviction" and won a financial settlement of $1.5 million. Soon after Kotler was released, he was arrested and convicted for committing a similar horrific crime. Needless to say, representatives from the Innocence Project do not like talking about the Kotler case. (Their Web site tersely claims that "He would later be convicted of different charges on the basis of DNA evidence.")

You won't be surprised to learn that the media gave little coverage to Kotler's new arrest and conviction, especially when compared to the mountains of press attention that followed his release upon exoneration. Such disparities in news coverage might not be such a big deal if they didn't cause such a serious public-safety problem. When exonerated-but-guilty men are released and mischaracterized as actually *innocent,* the public is unaware of their need to be vigilant, to protect themselves and their children against recidivist violence. The exonerated-but-guilty status means these guys are not on parole or probation. The government just lets them out and, as I mentioned, often hands them tons of taxpayer money, too, as a financial "apology"! A media frenzy celebrates their release from confinement. And then they're off—to start raping or killing again.

Even more disturbing is the fact that some of the stories of these so-called innocent men involve claims of money changing hands or other alleged bargains, to persuade people to make false confessions or fraudulently claim sole responsibility for the crime. This can be powerful evidence in support of the man professing his innocence because there's nothing more persuasive, either in a real court or in the court of public opinion, than having someone else confess to the crime. But a closer look at these confessions raises important questions about whether there might not be more to these stories.

For one thing, isn't it at least a startling coincidence that in a few celebrated cases the confessor who claims to have acted alone was found in prison by a guy proclaiming his innocence? And isn't it interesting that the discovery was made at a point in time when both the confessor and the allegedly innocent guy just happened to be spending time together behind bars in the same prison? Hmmmmm: makes you stop and think. Pure co-incidence, or a transparent case of deal making? Did the guy claiming innocence offer the false confessor a reward of some sort—maybe a piece of the settlement when he wins his lawsuit against the state for his wrongful conviction? A guy in prison might be willing to take sole responsibility for a crime—even if it means he might do extra time behind bars—if it creates a substantial benefit for him, such as a big pile of money that he can use for himself or give to his family on the outside. The most important question is, why doesn't anybody think it's worth looking at the money/influence trail to see whether there's some "there" there?

In at least one case, there's a specific claim of bribery. A guy named Alstory Simon says he was offered money on behalf of a convicted killer to say he acted alone in committing a crime. In 1998, Simon confessed to a murder for which a man named An-thony Porter had already been convicted and was on death row awaiting execution. Simon claimed he was the real killer and that Porter was completely innocent. This led to Porter's celebrated release from prison. Seven years later, Simon recanted his confes-sion, claiming he had falsely admitted to the crime after receiv-ing promises of lenient punishment as well as money and other rewards from book and movie deals about Porter's rescue from death row. The truth about all this remains murky, but, at the very least, claims that a man would be offered money to falsely confess to murder (and would take it) are extremely disturbing.

Thanks to people like Josh Marquis, the public is becoming appropriately skeptical. People are starting to understand that DNA rarely tells the whole story, even when it establishes the presence of an individual's body fluid at a certain location. Don't forget that O. J. Simpson's lawyers claimed that the presence of Ron Goldman's blood in Simpson's notorious white Bronco didn't necessarily prove Simpson's involvement in Goldman's murder. Well, um; okay. But the point is that if there had been an innocent explanation for that blood, it would be fair to say the evidence didn't necessarily prove Simpson's guilt.

The downside of all this DNA-lying is that the public ends up with the false impression that our criminal justice system desperately needs to make things better for accused criminals. And in truth, if the numbers of wrongly convicted innocent men were as high as the DNA lies suggest, it would be appropriate to spend time and resources studying and fixing relevant systemic flaws. But because the number of innocent, wrongly convicted men is actually minuscule (something like .0001 percent) compared to the countless defendants who are wrongly acquitted and the millions of criminals who are guilty but never charged—it simply isn't reasonable to waste precious resources trying to make the system perfect.

And guess what? The system will never be perfect from the perspective of the accused, and there's precious little that anyone can do about it. The very nature of the jury system means that human beings make decisions based on inherently imperfect sensory observations recounted by witnesses in the courtroom.

Some cases must be decided on the testimony of a single eyewitness. Why? Because that's all there is. This isn't the result of a flawed legal system but the natural by-product of crime. Criminals try hard not to get caught. They tend not to leave behind a mountain of incriminating evidence if they can avoid it. If the only evidence available to the prosecutor is the testimony of one eyewitness, and the jury believes that person beyond a reasonable doubt, the accused should be found guilty, period. This is no guarantee of perfection but it's far better than doing nothing based on the silly idea that a fair trial cannot be had in the absence of DNA evidence.

Lies about DNA have also unfairly influenced the death-penalty debate, because abolitionists have latched onto claims about countless innocent men being convicted as a reason to abolish capital punishment altogether. They argue that the wrongful execution of even one innocent man is too high a price to pay. Well, some honest observers might disagree with that conclusion. But the more important fact is that there is absolutely no proof that an innocent man has ever been executed. Ever. This is a pretty good track record. It hardly militates in favor of abolishing the death penalty.

Don't get me wrong. I'm personally opposed to the death penalty. But it's not right that some people are changing their minds about the issue based on false information about the numbers of truly innocent men who are being wrongly convicted. I believe that when the truth comes out about the DNA lies, voters will revert back to a pro-death-penalty position with a vengeance because nobody likes being tricked into changing their mind on such an important issue. As someone who can't accept the idea that the government should kill a human being as punishment, I don't look forward to that day.

DNA testing holds great promise as a tool that can help identify the guilty and vindicate the innocent. It's a good thing that tests are less expensive to conduct and can be done more quickly today than ever before. But it's no panacea, and we need to use this powerful scientific tool with our eyes wide open. It's too easy to be blinded by the gobbledygook of science and to passively accept as true claims that are difficult to rebut because the information is too complicated.

It's time to put an end to DNA lies. We need more intelligent responses to claims of innocence in court, and we need more balance and truth telling about these cases in the media, including having just as much coverage dedicated to the cases where DNA confirms a victim's credibility as there is coverage when DNA purportedly exonerates a suspect. For example, when a blind woman in Wisconsin, named in the press only as Patty, was raped at knifepoint in 1997, she couldn't identify her rapist. Police were so cruel to her they not only doubted her credibility, they charged her with lying about the crime even though she'd gone to the hospital and submitted to a rape exam where DNA evidence was taken. In 2001, that DNA was matched to a convicted sex offender named Joseph Bong; and police, to their credit, apologized to Patty. They also paid her $35,000 to settle the lawsuit she filed against them. Thirty-five thousand dollars? Many factually guilty but exonerated rapists get six-figure settlements when they sue for their wrongful convictions. Patty got a token sum and, believe me, she suffered far more than any guilty rapist ever did sitting in prison for a crime he really *did* commit. Maybe even worse than the insultingly low settlement is the fact that the media paid almost no attention to the case. There were no front-page stories in the big newspapers. No laudatory press conferences to showcase the power of DNA to prove a man's guilt and to vindicate Patty, the victim. Nothing at all, really. Just a couple of small stories. We need better balance in the stories.

Until then, you can take a stand. Be openly critical of defense attorneys who lie about DNA evidence. Be a skeptical consumer of news. When you read the word "exonerated," stop and ask yourself whether that means "actual innocence." For guidance on how to figure out the answer, check out the work of Dudley Sharp, who wrote a brilliant analysis of the misleading use of the words "exonerated" and "innocence" in the context of the death penalty. Write letters to the editors of print media who don't ask tough questions or who don't understand or who don't write honestly about whether "exonerated" means the same thing as "innocent." Hold your elected officials responsible by voting for candidates who will pass tough laws to prevent the waste of tax dollars on

1) expensive DNA tests that stand to violate a victim's privacy without any hope of proving a defendant's innocence
2) unfair lawsuits based on false claims of a convicted criminal's actual innocence.

Finally, be a smart citizen when you get called for jury duty. Try hard not to be overly impressed by evidence just because it's complicated or scientific. As citizens beholden to the task of doing justice, we have to stand firm and confident in our ability to apply common sense and see the truth in every criminal trial—no matter how distracting the razzle-dazzle of DNA science.

THREE

Victory Through Intimidation

HERE'S A BAD ONE: VICTIMS AND WITNESSES LITER-
ally walk away from criminal prosecutions because they've been
harassed, threatened, or pressured by either the perpetrator, his
buddies, or even his lawyer. I call it victory through intimidation. It happens in all kinds of cases, and in a variety of different
ways.

Witnesses to gang violence are regularly warned that they
will be hurt or killed if they cooperate with police. Organized
crime thugs have been killing off witnesses since before they
had to worry about courtrooms (in the spirit of not leaving any
loose ends behind). So witness intimidation isn't exactly new.

But things are a whole lot worse today because of how bold and widespread these tactics are and because so much intimidation occurs with the blessing (or at least the tacit cooperation) of the justice system.

In 2005, for example, gang members started wearing STOP SNITCHING T-shirts in and around Boston courtrooms as a mute but malevolent reminder to witnesses that they would be in danger if they told the truth. No, this isn't just some sick manifestation of gang loyalty; it is a tactic specifically calculated to help the bad guys go free by making the witnesses afraid to speak. Period. Does anybody in the courtroom do anything about it? No. Why? Because they're afraid that the ACLU will file a lawsuit claiming that STOP SNITCHING T-shirts are protected by the First Amendment. But what about the fact that victims and witnesses have a constitutional right to participate in judicial proceedings without intimidation? And what about the fact that the public has a right to everyone's testimony? These things don't seem to matter very much, so the barely veiled threats and the gang violence continue, hidden behind the noble robes of free speech.

Approximately 40 percent of murders in Massachusetts went unsolved in 2005. This is pretty good evidence that STOP SNITCHING T-shirts and similar tactics are working—and that the justice system isn't.

Another common intimidating tactic occurs when defense attorneys exclude parents from the courtroom when a child victim of abuse testifies against a perpetrator. In the 2001 Massachusetts prosecution of Daniel Miller, who was up for repeatedly sexually abusing a little boy (a case in which I was involved as an attorney for the victim), the child's parents were forced to sit outside the courtroom because the defense attorney, Michael Bourbeau, told the court he intended to call the parents as witnesses.

The parents desperately wanted to be in the room to comfort their child with their presence as he confronted the monster charged with assaulting him. Bourbeau claimed, however, that the parents' testimony would be tainted by what they heard while the child was on the stand, so they were locked out.

As I expected, the parents were never called by the defense. But with his mom and dad out of the room, the victim was all alone and terrified when he had to sit only a short distance from his attacker and tell a group of strangers about the terrible things that had happened to him.

Miller was acquitted. The tactic worked. The justice system didn't.

In another Massachusetts case in which I was involved as an attorney for the victim, in 2002, defense attorney Judith Lindahl sent several subpoenas to various medical professionals who provided care to a minor rape victim before and after the incident in question. A lower-court judge allowed the request, as a result of which, voluminous files were delivered to the court; files that contained reams of irrelevant, sensitive information about the victim and other family members, including her parents.

Is it ever appropriate to violate a victim's privacy rights? Reasonable minds can disagree. In this case, however, the intrusion was outrageous because the victim was under the age of consent; and there was DNA evidence that corroborated the victim's testimony and established that the perpetrator had sexual contact with the victim. In other words, violating the privacy of the victim served no purpose because the only fact that mattered—whether a sex act had occurred—had been established by objective science; and nothing in the records could possibly alter this fact. Even if, hypothetically, the records showed the victim had a severe mental illness, or a long pattern of false rape claims, nothing could have materially affected the significance of the DNA evidence. When a victim is too young to consent, the only evidence a prosecutor needs is proof that a sex act occurred. Period.

No, this certainly doesn't mean that the victim's credibility can't be challenged by the defense. But when credibility is relatively inconsequential, it is especially inappropriate to violate a (minor) victim's privacy. And whatever you think about the defense asking for a minor victim's personal files, it is unconscionable in the extreme to allow the defense to violate the parents' privacy rights. The parents had absolutely nothing to do with the crime; all they did was support their daughter in her quest for justice. And for this, they deserved to have defense attorneys, judges, and investigators tromping all over their privacy rights? I don't think so.

An appeal to a justice of the Massachusetts Supreme Judicial Court later that year was unavailing. The judge assigned to the case, Martha Sosman (who has since passed away), expressed little concern for the gratuitous damage to the privacy rights of the victim and her parents. In fact, Justice Sosman was already on record as believing that the law should permit virtually automatic access to the private records of rape victims. This wasn't the law at the time, but it was Justice Sosman's expressed intention to change the law to the substantial benefit of accused criminals, a change that would be to the detriment of victims. In my opinion, this clouded her capacity not only to judge the facts fairly but also to see how intimidating it was for her to allow an entire family to suffer the indignities of needless harm at the hands of an attorney for an accused rapist, especially when all they did was cooperate with law enforcement in the investigation and prosecution of a serious crime.

The family ultimately walked away from the case to avoid additional harm. The charges were dismissed.

In another of my cases—the 2003 criminal rape prosecution of a defendant named Manuel Valverde—defense attorney Paul Rudof did something similar. Rudof insisted on the full disclosure of a rape victim's crisis counseling file, while openly conceding that he had no idea what was in the file, why he needed it, or how violating the victim's privacy was necessary to protect his client's rights. Even worse is the way Rudof found out that the victim sought counseling services. His private investigator—again, paid for by public tax dollars—repeatedly contacted and harassed the victim's grandmother (her legal guardian at the time) to ask probing questions about personal issues. Like what? Well, like whether the victim had ever received counseling, whether the victim had ever been abused by anyone in the past, and whether the grandmother herself had ever been in jail or had been involved with the criminal justice system.

The investigator persisted in contacting the grandmother even after she said she did not want to talk. On one occasion when the grandmother was sick, lying on a sofa, the investigator again came to her home. To stop the harassment she finally relented and told the investigator that her granddaughter sought counseling after the rape at a local crisis center.

The victim's grandmother later explained to the court that she had no idea she had the right not to be harassed or not to answer questions posed by the investigator. The grandmother became tearful when she was told her answers were helping the defense attorney gain access to the victim's privileged counseling file. The victim was devastated; her grandmother was heartbroken.

Rather than punishing the defense, the judge ordered the crisis center to turn over the victim's file. When the center refused, citing the victim's privilege of confidentiality, the fact that the defense made no showing of need for the file, and the harassment of the victim's grandmother, the judge held the center in contempt and ordered them to pay a fine of $500 per day until they complied with the order.

The crisis center couldn't afford one day's fine, much less the fines that would be incurred during an appeal process, so I filed an emergency motion with an appellate judge. The media was covering the case, thankfully, and the public became so angry about what was happening to the victim and the crisis center that five hundred people signed a petition offering to spend one night in jail each in lieu of the fine. All five hundred names were attached to the appellate pleadings in a spreadsheet prepared by Irene Weiser at Stop Family Violence. Irene would eventually receive thousands of signatures from angry citizens willing to go to jail in order to stop this injustice.

It worked for a while: We won an initial stay of the fine and it helped that the *New York Times* covered the case. But when the public protest died down months later, the court ruled against us. This was not unexpected because several (but not all) appellate judges in Massachusetts just don't like the idea that victims hire lawyers and fight for their rights. But it is an important lesson in the value of public protest. When the public makes a lot of noise, the courts are less inclined to do the wrong thing.

Some defense attorneys send subpoenas for a specifically identified important piece of evidence that they know exists in a certain location. This is fine at the time of trial when cross-examination rights ripen in a constitutional sense and the defense is not seeking sensitive information. But fishing expeditions before trial are always wrong and some records, like privileged counseling files, should always be off limits because people who have been victimized have a fundamental right to heal in peace and safety.

Defense attorneys complain that privacy rights have to give way because "you never know" what might be in someone's personal files. Well, couldn't you say that about every witness in every case? Imagine that you are in line at a bank, and you see a man commit an armed robbery. You give a statement to police and later you tell your spouse about what you saw. If your spouse writes about your experience in a diary, should the robber be allowed to subpoena the diary on the theory "you never know" what might be in there? What if instead of telling your spouse, you tell your priest or your personal lawyer? Should those files be released so the defense can conduct a fishing expedition under the "you never know" rule? The truth is, such files virtually never prove a man's innocence, but almost always cause needless harm to victims.

Some argue that the accused has a constitutional right to conduct fishing expeditions. This is absolutely false. What they're really talking about is the so-called discovery process, where both sides have equal rights to ask each other for information. But discovery is primarily a civil-law, rather than a criminal-law, concept. And to the extent the accused has a right to discovery in a criminal matter, it applies only to evidence under the control of his opponent, the prosecutor. The simple fact is, there's no such thing as an accused criminal having a constitutional right to conduct discovery against private citizens, even for something as benign as grocery receipts, much less confidential files.

In criminal cases, the accused has rights against the government—but victims and witnesses are not parties to the criminal case. They don't bring the charges and they're not the defendant's opponent. The accused receives what is labeled discovery from the prosecutor because the government has a constitutional obligation to share its investigative file with the defense.

Although the law is clear that there is no constitutional right to send discovery subpoenas to private citizens, in Massachusetts and a few other states, many judges aren't paying attention. They let defense attorneys run roughshod all over the rights of people who have done nothing wrong and have suffered enough.

Too many defense attorneys send subpoenas for victims' private records simply because they know damn well that many people are intimidated by subpoenas, so they roll over and comply, even if the subpoena is illegal. Some victims take the opposite approach. They are so insulted they just walk away from the case altogether. To a defense attorney, that's a victory. To me, it's a disgrace. It's why I started fighting for victims in the first place.

Back in 1992, I generated my first test case in an attempt to change the law and better protect victims' privacy rights. I advised a crisis center to refuse to comply with a subpoena for a victim's records. The judge held the center in contempt, and we filed an appeal that generated a lot of public support. When it got to the point where it looked like we were going to win our appeal and change the law, the strangest thing happened: The public defender, Catherine Byrne, had the accused rapist plead guilty and the next thing I knew, the judge was declaring our appeal moot.

Here's what's interesting about this. The guy was out on very low bail; he would have stayed out of jail for at least another year while our appeal was being decided. And suddenly he was willing to plead guilty and go to prison for eight to ten years—and this just happened to have the effect of threatening to destroy our opportunity to change the law. It seemed clear to me this was a direct assault on our appeal. Could the liberty of Byrnes's client have taken a backseat to her ideological agenda?

This isn't the only time I've been suspicious of attempts to prevent a victim's or a prosecutor's appeal as a ploy to prevent the law from changing to the benefit of victims. But it's an important story because it helps explain why defense lawyers have so much control over the evolution of criminal law in general. Not only do defense lawyers often head up key criminal justice committees in state legislatures, they control powerful rule-making boards, where decisions are made that affect constitutional and criminal law policy issues. The defense bar can also cherry-pick the issues they bring to the attention of appellate courts while thwarting the efforts of lawyers like me who are trying to repair some of the problems that plague victims.

It's even worse in some states, like Massachusetts, where prosecutors rarely pursue their own appeals because it's simply too expensive. It's actually doubly expensive compared to the cost imposed on public defenders' budgets because, win or lose, when prosecutors appeal, they are forced to pay not only their own costs, but the costs of the defense, as well. In many cases, we're talking about *your* tax dollars being used to create a financial disincentive for prosecutors to correct injustices. Did you know your money was working to silence victims' voices in the development of criminal law policy?

Despite defense attempts to moot my 1992 appeal, the court let our case continue, and we ultimately won a huge victory when the court agreed with us that the law had to be changed.

Despite this victory, it was clear to me that the court was uncomfortable having a private lawyer representing a victim in a criminal case. It didn't matter that the court fixed a terrible injustice that I brought to their attention, which obviously was something I couldn't have accomplished without doing exactly that: serving as a private attorney for a victim in a criminal case. I knew they weren't thrilled with what I had done because they agreed with my argument—but announced their decision to change the law in someone else's case.

I know what I think of that. What do you think of that?

For my part, I didn't give a damn about the lost glory. What mattered was winning, not getting credit for the win. (The press figured it out, so I got the credit anyway.) But in the wake of this bizarre chain of events, I knew I had to make an important decision. Should I continue with the type of work that was so obviously important to victims, or should I move on to the "real world" of lawyering and avoid controversy?

I chose to continue working for victims. They need all the help they can get, and not too many people are volunteering for the job.

Based on my experience over the past twenty years or so, it's clear I made the right decision. I've helped lots of victims protect themselves from "victory through intimidation." But more needs to be done. First, we need to send a zero-tolerance message to the types of wayward defense attorneys who use illegal subpoenas and engage in tactics like allowing grandmothers to be harassed by private investigators. They should be punished with mandatory economic and licensing sanctions for the first offense—and worse if they don't get the message the first time.

We also need, in every state, an entity where victims can go to report defense attorney misconduct. The best model today, combining oversight and accountability, is the Alaska Office on Victims' Rights (AOVR). The AOVR functions something like an inspector general's office. When a victim's rights are violated, an investigator can issue subpoenas and interrogate individuals to determine whether punishment is appropriate. For example, under Alaska law, all defense interviews with victims must be recorded and victims must be advised of their right not to answer questions. If this is not done, a victim can file a complaint with the AOVR. Attorneys who engage in improper tactics can then be identified in a public report published annually by the AOVR. No, it's not much of a stick, but in conjunction with economic and licensing sanctions, it's substantially better than what most states have now, which is nothing.

Another important remedy, as I mentioned in Chapter 1, involves regular auditing of public defenders' budgets to make sure the system isn't wasting tax money on overpayments to lawyers and private investigators who are using public dollars to intimidate crime victims and their families.

We also need more legal support for victims who refuse to comply with unjust subpoenas and court orders. By allowing more third-party objections in court, victims can fight back better and help bring public awareness to intimidation tactics in criminal cases.

Finally, victims need to consider filing lawsuits against unethical defense attorneys and defense investigators. I don't say this lightly and it shouldn't be done often. When I did it, not only did the individual lawyer I targeted stop sending unlawful subpoenas, but when other attorneys found out he'd been successfully sued, they stopped doing it, too. Yes, lawsuits can be abused, and we have to be vigilant against that. But a well-chosen and vigorously pursued lawsuit can serve as a highly effective kind of quality-control device—one that inspires better behavior from attorneys who wouldn't otherwise give a damn about the rules.

Four

Race Baiting

WHEN THE NAME OF THE GAME IS DEFENSE AT ANY cost, truth doesn't matter. Nor does exploiting prejudice, even when the collateral damage to our social fabric is enormous.

For certain types of defense attorneys, there are no limits. Playing the race card or the gender card is perfectly acceptable because—as they see it—justice itself is irrelevant during a criminal trial. Forget truth and fairness; winning is the only goal. For them, it's all about putting another notch in the belt. It's about bragging rights at the local pub, where defense lawyers one-up each other with tales of the latest vile trick they've used to get a guilty criminal off scot-free.

Think I'm exaggerating? I'm not. O. J. Simpson is a free man today because his lawyers played the defense-at-any-cost game by using the race card in a massive, relentless way, convincing the jurors that the loathsome Simpson was only in the docket because a bunch of racists had it in for him. Forget all that evidence; it was all about prejudice.

Make no mistake about it: Defense attorneys will gladly whip jurors into a frenzy over a hot-button social issue—any hot-button social issue—if they believe that this tactic will divert attention away from the real evidence and help even the most dangerous criminal walk free.

Kobe Bryant's lawyer, Pamela Mackey, did it when she held forth in open court in January 2004 that "there is lots of history about black men being falsely accused of this crime by white women." Note that Mackey played two cards at once—race and gender—a neat trick that gets twice the bang for half the buck because a lot of people don't even notice the gender card. Gender bias is so pervasive and so passively accepted in rape cases that using sexism against the victim isn't even seen as playing a card, much less an offensive bigoted one. So mixing race and gender bias to claim that white women have a history of falsely accusing black men of rape worked effectively to ignite a big fire under people watching a high-profile trial unfold.

Forget that research shows almost all rapes occur between people of the same race; that the false-allegation rate is minuscule (people are far more likely to falsely report their own death); and that while some women do make false charges, there is no evidence that false allegations are disproportionately made by white women against black men. When it comes to racism and sexism, myths trump truth.

I think you could make the case that of all the despicable tactics described in this book, race baiting is the most destructive to society. Can helping one man win a criminal trial be worth causing major damage to race relations across an entire nation? I think it's a question worth asking. But Kobe Bryant's and O. J. Simpson's lawyers simply didn't care. Simpson's lawyers knew that if the jury heard Mark Fuhrman, the detective on the case, use the N-word, the facts about the murders wouldn't matter; and Bryant's lawyers knew that invoking images of black men being lynched in the antebellum South would have people talking more about slavery than the allegations of rape. Race baiting in Simpson's case was so effective, it dragged jurors' attention away from mountains of DNA and other circumstantial evidence that should have proved Simpson's guilt beyond any doubt, thereby proving the theory that the more powerful the prosecution's case, the bigger the distraction has to be—and the prosecution's case against Simpson was damn strong.

No judge in his right mind permits the strategic exploitation of race discrimination (or other kinds of prejudice) as a trial strategy. Judge Ruckreigle, in Bryant's case, should have held Mackey in contempt for making such an idiotic and incendiary statement, and Judge Lance Ito should have ruled that Fuhrman's use of the N-word was, as a matter of fact and law, irrelevant. The day he caved to the pressure and allowed the N-word testimony, the case was over. So what in the world was he thinking? Well, let's not forget that there were angry crowds outside the courthouse almost every day throughout Simpson's trial. Why were they there? In part because of the cynical and racially insensitive tactics of the defense team. Ito apparently concluded that he simply couldn't get away with making the right ruling. A double murderer walked away scot-free, not because the prosecution failed to prove its case but because defense attorney F. Lee Bailey and his colleagues agreed to spew racial venom in the courtroom.

My question is: How exactly do we get the F. Lee Baileys of the world to pay back society for the harm they cause to racial harmony in this country? And more important, how do we stop another generation of junior F. Lee Baileys from doing the same thing in the future?

It won't be easy, in part because there are many more Bailey types out there. Take, for example, defense attorney Robert George, who adopted pretty much the same strategy in the Cape Cod trial of a black man named Christopher McCowen. McCowen was prosecuted for the murder of socialite Christa Worthington, who was stabbed to death in her home in the remote oceanside town of Truro, Massachusetts. Police solved the crime when they identified the DNA found in Worthington's genital area as belonging to McCowen, who was Worthington's garbage man. McCowen all but confessed to the crime, telling police he had sex with her and beat her but didn't kill her. He then claimed that a friend of his stabbed the victim. Unfortunately for McCowen, his intended fall guy had a solid alibi. When McCowen was told that his friend couldn't possibly have done it, he replied that he realized he alone would likely be held accountable.

Attorney George argued to the jury that because his client is black, police and prosecutors were racist for arresting his client. He claimed that racism had led the police to arrest his client because they simply couldn't accept the reality of a white socialite having consensual sex with a black garbage man. Of course, George conveniently left out the fact that his client had more or less confessed to the heinous crime. But my point is that there's nothing racist about police concluding the killer was, indeed, the guy who admitted to whacking the victim around and whose DNA just happened to be found in her body.

But George didn't stop at gratuitously accusing the police of racism. He also engaged in his own pernicious brand of racism and sexism by telling the jury that they should believe Worthington had consensual sex with McCowen because she had a history of engaging in sex acts with social undesirables. It's astounding, if you think about it. After complaining that McCowen was only in trouble because the cops were racist, George himself labeled his client a social undesirable. Because he was . . . poor? A garbage man? Black?

The silence from antiracism activists was deafening. True, I, and a few people like me did complain about George's race-baiting strategy. At the same time, though, I heard a number of defense attorneys arguing George had a right to exploit social prejudice to help his client win, whether it was legitimately an issue in the case or not.

I find this unbelievable. What do you think?

Certain criminal-defense types think winning a case by making people hate each other based on race is something to be proud of.

But it isn't.

The system badly needs an overhaul to deal with the manipulation of prejudice as a trial tactic. One solution is what is known in California as the snitch rule. The idea grew out of public disgust with the O. J. Simpson verdict. It simply requires jurors to rat out other jurors who refuse to deliberate honestly, or who render decisions based on improper criteria. In other words, a juror who says, "I'm voting 'not guilty' because I want to cut the defendant some slack as a black man" would be removed from jury service. So would the juror who declares, "I'm voting 'guilty' because the defendant is a black man." These are both highly improper criteria, and any juror who resorted to one of them would be bounced. Justice demands exactly that outcome.

Prosecutors also need to fight for the right to appeal unjust acquittals when the result is directly caused by discrimination against a particular social class. I understand that this might require a constitutional amendment, which of course would take a long time and a lot of effort. But someone needs to get the ball rolling before we embarrass ourselves again on the world stage with another O. J. fiasco.

It would help if we had better screening of jurors for all types of serious biases, and not just those that might disadvantage the accused. In 2005, the jurors in the Michael Jackson case were screened for race prejudice, which of course is a good thing. They were also screened to determine whether they or anyone close to them had ever been abused as a child. This was supposed to make sure the juror wouldn't be too sympathetic to the victim, but is this question really fair? Many people are close to someone who was abused as a child, but this doesn't necessarily make them people who can't judge child-abuse cases with due regard for the rights of the accused. In fact, it probably makes them particularly good jurors in these cases because they have a better understanding of the evidence. There is no scientific research showing that jurors who are friendly with people who have been victimized are inherently less fair to defendants than jurors who don't have such friends. Doesn't seem to matter.

While the potentially sympathetic jurors were being screened out in Jackson's case, nobody was asking a single question of the jurors to determine whether they, or anyone close to them, had ever molested a child, or were members of any organization—say the North American Man/Boy Love Association (NAMBLA)—that might bend their view in a certain direction. Did the absence of such screening affect the jury's decision to acquit? We'll never know. But we do need laws that mandate bumping NAMBLA members, and people like them, out of child–sex abuse trials. The form of prejudice against kids that NAMBLA embodies does as much harm to the justice system as race baiting, because it's a type of bias that legitimizes violence. How can we claim that prejudice has no place in a fair legal system and yet do absolutely nothing to exclude these people from jury service in cases where they believe the crime charged is a form of affection?

Here's the bottom line: Prejudice in the courtroom is always unacceptable—no matter which side it helps or hurts—because it perpetuates prejudice in the real world. Think of all the role models in our society—the teachers, spiritual leaders, business people, and politicians—who work so hard every day to fight discrimination in our society. Are we being fair to them? Are we honoring their noble work when we let defense attorneys fan the flames of prejudice with impunity, for selfish strategic reasons aimed at helping a guilty criminal walk free?

I don't think so.

FIVE

Winning Through Payoffs and Extortion

IT'S CERTAINLY NOT NEWS THAT RICH CRIMINALS GET better treatment than poor ones. Maybe that's just one of those realities that we can talk about and fight against but never quite eliminate. I can accept that life in general is almost always easier for people with a lot of money.

But for our purposes in this chapter, we have to go down another level. Benefiting from wealth is one thing. Corrupting justice with payoffs and extortion is a whole other kettle of fish. Yes, money can and does buy the best lawyer—and that's fine— but money shouldn't be able to buy witnesses or the dismissal of criminal charges.

Yet payoffs and extortion seem downright commonplace in today's criminal justice system. Every time you turn around, there's another story about a key witness in a criminal case simply not showing up for trial. And all too often, you hear about some critical piece of evidence in a trial that's gone missing, or has somehow become tainted. People rarely ask why this is so—much less insist on an investigation to determine whether some form of corruption is afoot.

So what's the message? I guess if you are are contemplating committing a crime, you should plan on getting rich first. The worst-and-wealthiest among us can essentially count on an acquittal based not on the weakness of the prosecution's case but on whether they have enough money to pad the pockets of the key witnesses, sufficient to make critical evidence disappear, which in turn will ensure that the whole case will go south. I know this sounds cynical, and maybe you're not even surprised. After all, phrases like "money walks" and "rich man's justice" have been around for a long time. But at least we used to complain about it. We used to think it was wrong and that someone should do something about it.

I'm not sure why we stopped caring, but think it started around the time Michael Jackson bought his way out of a criminal prosecution in 1993 by lining the pockets of his victim. How much did Jackson have to spend to thwart justice back then? The answer, reportedly, is between $15 million and $20 million. This is an ungodly sum of money for even the superrich to pony up. Such a whopper of a payoff suggests that the evidence was truly of blockbuster quality. And as we later found out, the clincher was reportedly testimony of unusual markings on Jackson's genitals—obviously something about which a child who hadn't been molested would have no way of knowing.

Lady Justice is supposed to be blind. In Michael Jackson's case, she was more like blind, deaf, and dumb pimp—facilitating a walk for Jackson when he should have been locked up for a long, long time. The guy was accused of child rape. (Yes, we can't shy away from it; it was rape. The allegations involved penile/oral penetration.) But after the payoff, the victim conveniently changed his tune from that of a cooperating witness to a victim who refused to testify.

Paying a victim for silence should be prosecuted as obstruction of justice and the lawyers who brokered these deals—including Johnny Cochran, who did it for Jackson, and Larry Feldman, who represented the victim—should have been treated as criminals, pure and simple.

Emboldened by his payoff "victory," Jackson flaunted his ability to molest kids with impunity by appearing in public with little boys in pajamas, writing a song taunting the frustrated prosecutor, and eventually boasting on international television that he often sleeps in his bed with little boys. Sometimes when I hear these stories, I picture the framers of our Constitution learning of this perverted outcome of their noble work. They wanted to ensure that accused criminals received due process, but I suspect they would cringe at visions of Jackson thumbing his fake nose at the justice system with one hand while grabbing the rear end of a little boy with the other. And I'm certain they would tear the document up and start over if they learned that O. J. Simpson made a small fortune on his vile book, *If I Did It,* where he hypothetically confesses to the murders of Ron Goldman and Nicole Brown and reveals for profit the mysterious details about how he "did it." The book was pulled before it reached bookstores, but Simpson still managed to pocket a reported six-figure sum because the publisher saw value in the revelation of details related to how and why Simpson would have slaughtered two innocent people. The most horrible part of this, aside from the grotesque idea that such a book could even be conceived, is that the value of Simpson's musings was created in part by our precious Fifth Amendment—a key constitutional provision that allows citizens to remain silent during police interrogations. Forcing an individual to become a witness against himself is anathema to the ideals of a free society. But while the Fifth Amendment facilitates the keeping of secrets by criminals, it should hardly be tolerated that the criminal can then trade on the value of the mystery by making a profit on the disclosure of the truth.

Can you see how sick and perverted this is? We have a Constitution that allows murderers to keep secrets about their crimes—to protect liberty for all of us—but we have nothing that effectively prevents acquitted murderers from turning the value of that secret into profit, literally exploiting the sacred nature of an essential freedom and using it like a stock share or a commodity to be traded and sold to the highest bidder. Sure, people were outraged, and the book was cancelled; but because Simpson was paid a ton of money up front, the damage to the Constitution was done. Shame on us. Shame on everyone who jerked a First Amendment knee rather than doing something—anything—to shut Simpson up, or at least make it painful, rather than profitable, for him to utter a single word about murdering Ron and Nicole.

What am I talking about? How about passing a law that imposes an automatic fine on Simpson whenever he says *anything* about the murders. Maybe this dents his First Amendment rights a bit, but so what? Some people deserve less freedom than the rest of us. And how about taking his kids away from him as punishment for abusing them by purporting to "confess" to the murder of their mother for profit. Parents routinely lose custody of their children for far less serious transgressions. But not Simpson. This guy goes to trial for the murder of his children's mother, walks away scot-free by exacerbating racism, loses a multimillion-dollar civil judgment, refuses to pay a dime while flaunting his wealth, then sells his supposed confession of the brutal details of his crimes for profit, claiming he did it to provide for his children's futures. And he still gets to be a father?

But should we really be surprised that Simpson got away with this behavior? In an anything-goes culture, Simpson had every reason to believe he could get away with writing a confession book for profit no matter how distasteful, and no matter how much harm it caused his children. After all, Michael Jackson had literally paid cash for a victim's silence and then flaunted that fact all over town, while continuing to engage in inappropriate activity with little boys. So why couldn't Simpson exploit the justice system for money in any way he damn well pleased? Why would anyone not think the sky's the limit when it comes to making lots of blood money?

Even the good guys didn't fight it when Jackson bought his way out of prosecution in the early 1990s. Everyone on all sides of the payoff, including the victim and his family, should hang their heads in shame for what happened with Jackson—and for the ripple effect that followed, including society's newfound tolerance for all forms of corruption and profiting in the criminal justice system. But the prosecutor, Tom Sneddon, who claimed to be angry about the Jackson payoff, bears some of the blame, too. He could have sent the victim a subpoena and forced him to testify, holding him in jail if necessary until he told the truth. Isn't that what we do when witnesses to bank robberies and gang violence resist testifying? Don't we want the heavy hand of government to prevent corruption and come down hard on serious crime? Isn't child sex abuse a serious crime?

We can't afford to have an exception that lets certain types of witnesses off the hook, so long as the perpetrator is rich enough and immoral enough to overwhelm their interest in justice. Justice should never be treated like a swap meet. I'll say it again. Justice has to be better than capitalism if we want people to respect the law and each other. A system that claims no preferences based on wealth will be much more effective protecting all kids, but especially poor kids, from the Michael Jacksons of the world.

Payoffs breed cynicism and mistrust. The fact that no charges were brought against Jackson in 1993 led some people to believe the charges were false, and that the whole investigation was rooted in racism. After all, they reasoned, no prosecutor worth his salt would have allowed a real child rapist to walk free. Or would he?

To truly protect people from violence in our communities, prosecutors have to turn a deaf ear to defense attorney types who argue that payoffs are a form of justice because at least the victim gets compensation for their suffering. Baloney. Victims can and must participate in the criminal justice system, and then sue the perpetrator for money if they want to. I represent victims in both types of cases all the time. There is no need to funnel money for a victim's injuries through a criminal case. Ignoring this obvious truth excuses the government for not getting the job done.

It's not only criminal lawyers who need to get this straight. Civil plaintiff lawyers deserve some of the blame for the corruption problem because they engage in the flip side of payoffs when they extort extra money to take advantage of the fact that the defendant wants to keep ugly information out of the public arena. What do I mean by this? When a case itself is worth little or nothing—but the scandal value is high—some plaintiff lawyers demand much more than the case is worth as a price for keeping the matter quiet. This is not good lawyering; it is extortion; and it is unethical; and it happens all the time.

Consider the lawyers who demanded more than $2 million from Bill Clinton to settle Paula Jones's claim that he sexually harassed her by pulling his pants down. Maybe it was a valid claim—who knows? But two million bucks? How scary is a penis? The case was worth $100,000 on its best day; the rest was pure extortion.

We have a right to expect more from our legal system. Extortion and other forms of improper or corrupt litigation strategies massively undercut the integrity of the process and destroy public faith in justice.

To fix this craziness, we need new laws that expressly forbid victims to have any control over whether charges are "dropped" after they're initiated by the government. I'm not saying that victims' feelings are irrelevant, or that if the choice is between testifying and death, giving testimony is always the top priority. It isn't. But dismissing criminal charges because the victim doesn't feel like testifying because he'd rather go shopping with his new wad of dough is flat-out wrong.

We also need new laws that require full public disclosure of the financial records of victims, witnesses, and defendants whenever evidence of corruption is apparent. If there was a payoff, we all have a right and a need to know about it and everyone involved should be prosecuted.

Finally, we need laws that forbid the filing of civil lawsuits until the related criminal case has ended. To protect everyone's rights, the ticking of the clock on the civil statute of limitations should be put on hold while the criminal case is pending. Holding off the filing of civil lawsuits will prevent things like what occurred in the Kobe Bryant case where the dismissal of the criminal charges just happened to follow the victim's refusal to testify. This refusal just happened to coincide with the settlement of a civil lawsuit that—as many people thought on the day the lawsuit was filed—looked a whole lot like a sham vehicle through which a payoff would ultimately occur. Shame on everyone who participated, including the victim. Taxpayers shelled out a small fortune getting the case ready for trial only to have the public's interest used as leverage to jack up the value of a civil lawsuit. The victim gets a windfall; the public gets screwed. She should have at least been ordered to use some of her private settlement to repay the people of Colorado for the time and money spent getting her case ready for trial. Most of all, shame on us for not having laws to prevent such a circus in the first place.

No, we won't ever flush all the money out of the system. But at least we can minimize the posting of JUSTICE FOR SALE signs and prevent the spread of infectious disrespect for the law that comes with passive acceptance of outright corruption.

SIX

Using Delay Strategically

ALMOST EVERYONE HAS HEARD OF THE "RIGHT TO A speedy trial." This was built into our legal system (in the Sixth and Fourteenth Amendments to the Constitution) by wise men who understood the dangers of letting a government seize people off the street, lock them up, and never quite get around to bringing them to trial. Freedom for all of us is protected in part by our constitutional right to a speedy (and public) trial.

Truly innocent people generally benefit from speeding things up. You get your freedom (and your life) back swiftly. You minimize your legal bills. You remove that cloud from over your head and restore your good name as quickly as possible.

But speedy trials are rarely demanded in most cases. Why would that be? Frankly, it's because more than 99 percent of formally accused criminals are guilty of something, and they sure don't want to rush their own personal Judgment Day. This is why the typical defendant asks not for a speedy trial but instead for the slowest damn trial he can possibly hold out for.

When cases get delayed, witnesses die and move away. Memories fade, emotions subside, and evidence gets lost. A good defense, like a good wine, gets better with age, as the old adage goes. Obviously, wine gets better for the drinker, and the defense gets better for the accused.

Let's examine whether the prosecution of Robert Blake, charged with the 2001 slaying of his wife, presents an odoriferous case in point. Blake was acquitted after the case was dragged out for years, in large part because Blake hired and/or fired four different lawyers to represent him. One lawyer after another quit or was fired, virtually on the eve of each trial date. His first two lawyers claimed they resigned after Blake did media interviews against their advice. His third lawyer, Thomas Mesereau, stepped down right before trial was to begin, citing "irreconcilable differences."

Who knows what this meant in Blake's particular case. Maybe Mesereau was telling the truth, but all too often, at least when I've seen this particular card played, "irreconcilable differences" means either that the defendant refused to pay his legal fees or that the lawyer and client agreed that citing "irreconcilable differences" will force the court to grant a delay in the trial. Most judges will give a lawyer newly assigned to a case lots of time to prepare—even if they are convinced that it's an inappropriate delay tactic. (Failure to do so, they believe, might open them up to a reversal upon appeal.)

But I'm sorry, Judge Schempp, a judge with guts would have told Blake to knock it off after the first lawyer was bumped. (We're talking about Superior Court Judge Darlene Schempp.) A judge with guts would have said, "You're going to trial next time even if you fire another lawyer. In fact, you will represent yourself if you pull this stunt again." Judge Schempp could have done this because there's no such thing as a constitutional right to keep firing lawyers until all the witnesses drop dead. But judges with backbone are hard to find these days—especially in high-profile cases.

Delay tactics have been going on for a very long time, so they're nothing new. But the illness seems to be spreading, and defense attorneys are bolder than ever at coming up with excuses for putting the brakes on justice. Some of the excuses are so lame it's a wonder the whole courtroom doesn't burst out laughing upon hearing them. It's like the old "my dog ate my homework" line, except that the excuses are usually even less plausible and the stakes are far higher.

Judges rarely raise a skeptical eyebrow, much less punish the defense—as they should—for causing needless delays. I remember one defense attorney, back when I was a prosecutor, who had an absolutely horrible reputation for lying about why he needed yet another delay in his cases. People in the courthouse used to joke about how his grandmother must have been a cat because he delayed his clients' trials to go to her funeral at least nine times. Funny enough, until you start to think about the devastating impact of these delays on victims, who usually can't begin to get on with their lives until the criminal case is finally over.

I recall vividly the day when a rape victim client said to me, just after her trial had been delayed, "If the defense attorney gets to drag this out one more time, I won't be able to handle it." She strongly implied that she might hurt herself. She had been under tremendous stress preparing for the trial, revisiting the terrible memories again, thinking hard about the worst experience of her life—the night a stranger broke into her dorm room and attacked her repeatedly at knifepoint. She was ready, nerves steeled and misgivings squelched, finally ready to face the man who brutalized her—only to have the judge send everyone home after Boston defense attorney Mary Ames got her wish and the trial was delayed. It was treated as cavalierly as if Ames asked to reschedule a dentist's appointment. The defendant caught a break while the victim literally suffered physical pain.

And there's no question the delay in that case cost taxpayers money. All delays waste time and money. Defense attorneys know this, and the ones driven by ideology know that by making prosecutions more expensive, fewer cases can be pursued, which—they believe, in some twisted corner of their minds—is somehow good for the Constitution. I'm serious about this. Many lawyers who do defense work are anti–law enforcement ideologues who believe that if they force the court system to waste time and money, they are somehow protecting civil liberties by preventing prosecutors from having enough resources to take on more cases.

We really could be doing a much more efficient job of prosecuting criminals if someone had the political will to put a stop to strategic delay. Tying the government's hands by jacking up the cost of each prosecution doesn't protect freedom for anyone. It actually hurts civil liberties because, by squeezing the justice system, people who try their best to respect the constitutional rights of criminals are forced to cut corners, and the due process rights of all accused criminals suffer. If defense attorneys really cared about freedom, they would do everything in their power to expedite trials to ensure that the system has the capacity to allow delays for those defendants who really need the extra time to prepare for and receive a fair trial. When the Robert Blakes of the world drag their cases out for no good reason, the poor defendants who can't afford to keep hiring and firing lawyers get short-changed. It's simple economics. People like Blake demand unfair advantages and basic fairness for everyone else takes a hit. I'm sure a bunch of guys in prison have a message for Robert Blake: Thanks a lot!

This kind of greedy abuse of the system was readily apparent in a recent case out of Pennsylvania, where a man was convicted of multiple sex crimes after what the court described as a "savage" assault. Evidence was "overwhelming," according to the court, that the perpetrator brutally raped an unconscious seventeen-year-old girl with a light bulb, a shot glass, and a hanger—in front of witnesses. After the conviction, the rapist's lawyer filed a massive appeal, raising 150 issues, most of which the court deemed frivolous.

The court was so disgusted by the ridiculously excessive number of claims on appeal, it wrote in its decision upholding the convictions that the defense attorney, Sara Webster, had egregiously violated her duty of good faith and fair dealing with the court. Appellate judge Mitchell Goldberg was clearly infuriated that the court was forced to waste enormous public resources on the case. He took the extraordinary, though appropriate, step of recommending that the perpetrator and his lawyer be punished for their blatant violation of the rules. Judge Goldberg should get an award. Other judges should take a lesson.

Let's look at one case in some depth to more forcefully make the point about abusive strategies that waste time and precious public resources. It's the case of Debra Hagen, who may be the most violated and exploited victim in the history of our court system when it comes to delay tactics in criminal cases.

Debra was a young woman in her twenties in 1985 when she was brutally raped by a close family friend she called her godfather, James Kelly. Kelly was convicted by a jury in 1987 and sentenced to serve ten years in state prison. But as of 2001, when Debra asked me to represent her, Kelly had yet to serve a day behind bars.

Like many crime victims, Debra assumed that the prosecutor was on her side. Big mistake, as Debra learned when the years went by and, despite many calls to the district attorney's office, Kelly remained out on the street. Debra became suspicious when she was told Kelly couldn't go to prison because he was ill. Other times, it was because Kelly's appeal was still pending. Debra didn't know if any of this was true, but what could she do? The lawyer who was supposed to be on her side just kept patting her on the head and telling her not to worry, the legal process was simply running its dreadfully slow course.

It pains me to say it, but Debra had faith in the system. She had done all the right things that were expected of her as a rape victim. She reported the crime to police right away. She then went to the hospital, where evidence was obtained and photographs were taken of the bruises on her neck. She cooperated with law enforcement, waited patiently during the grueling pretrial period, and ultimately testified in front of a jury about all the horrible details.

When Kelly's trial wrapped up in 1987, the jury found him guilty almost immediately. The judge was prepared right then and there to pronounce sentence, but Kelly suddenly appeared to become faint in the courtroom. Sentencing was put off, and Kelly was admitted to a psychiatric ward at a local hospital.

Kelly finally showed up to receive his punishment months later, arriving by ambulance after another alleged medical problem. The judge sentenced him to prison, but put a hold on Kelly's incarceration until he got out of the hospital.

It was the government's job to have someone waiting to take Kelly to prison the minute he left the hospital. But somehow that didn't happen. Instead, a convicted rapist went home to freedom.

Debra called the prosecutor many times over the years to ask why Kelly was still free. In 1992, she even sent a letter to the judge seeking an explanation, but the judge passed it on to the prosecutor—and nothing happened.

In fact, the prosecution continued to do nothing for ten more years until police happened upon Kelly one day and realized he should have been behind bars. The local media caught on and started writing stories about the nearly-fourteen-year delay. The elected prosecutor, District Attorney John Conte, was desperate to make the whole thing go away as quickly as possible.

When I came on board, Conte's office was trying to get Debra to agree to a deal that would allow Kelly to avoid prison. The public would be outraged, but if it was at Debra's request, the prosecutor could get rid of the case altogether by claiming he only made the deal out of respect for Debra's wishes.

Debra, to her eternal credit, simply would not be used. She wanted Kelly to serve the sentence he had justly received—nothing more, nothing less. And she wanted some accountability for the fourteen years of delay. I filed papers with the judge as Debra's private lawyer, citing her right under Massachusetts law to a "prompt disposition," and asking the court to do exactly as Debra asked: Make Kelly start serving his sentence and tell her the truth about what took so long.

At the hearing on our motion, Kelly arrived in a wheelchair, slouched over and drooling. Though Kelly was now in his seventies and he looked feeble, I was intensely suspicious, because odd claims about his poor health were all over the case file.

The next day, a local newspaper published a front-page photo of Kelly in his wheelchair and wrote a sympathetic story implying that Debra was cruel for demanding that such a sick old man go to prison. That same day, I received information from police and others that Kelly was, in fact, a pretty healthy guy. He had a girlfriend and had recently been observed walking, smoking, driving his car, and so on.

But even if Kelly had been ill, so what? Since when is there an illness exception to incarceration? Criminals far sicker than

Kelly pretended to be are sent to prison all the time. I once prosecuted an eighty-eight-year-old man for second-offense child–sexual abuse—a crime that carried a five-year mandatory minimum prison term—after he molested a child from his bed in a nursing home. He always came to court using a walker, and his lawyer complained it was inhumane to put such an old man behind bars. Give me a break! If a perp is healthy enough to coerce a little girl visiting Nana at the rest home to fondle his penis, he's more than healthy enough to have his whole evil body shipped off to prison—walker and all.

Growing doubts about Kelly's disabilities led a *Boston Herald* reporter, Jack Sullivan, to stake out Kelly's home. In the course of the stake-out, Kelly was photographed smoking, weeding his garden, and taking out large bags of trash. No drooling, frail old man—just a fraud caught in the act. And as the icing on the cake, the prosecutor—the guy who was supposed to be helping Debra—was doing almost nothing to stop the scam.

Thanks to Jack Sullivan, the court and the public could finally see Kelly for the devious trickster he was—a master manipulator whose charade was being aided by lawyers, which made the whole mess much, much worse.

With the help of an attorney who put her interests first, Debra managed to shine a light on a terrible injustice, while teaching others about the harm that is imposed on all victims when justice is delayed.

Debra's perseverance paid off. Not only did Kelly go to prison—where he died—Debra's case led to new laws that reinforce the right of all crime victims to stand up in court and directly address the judge to demand speedy justice.

Debra's struggle is a tale of prosecutorial laziness, intimidation tactics, outrageous lies, and blatant unfairness facilitated by strategically engineered delays that almost succeeded in letting a convicted rapist avoid punishment for the brutal rape of a young woman. The remedy for Debra did not require complicated legislation and the appointment of commissions to study the problem, as is all too often the response when the government gets caught with its pants down. What Debra did is what any one of us should do if faced with the same situation: She persevered and stood firm until justice was served. For fifteen years, Debra simply refused to go away until the right thing was done and Kelly was behind bars. As you can probably tell, I have immense admiration for her strength and commitment to such an important cause.

Yes, defendants are owed a speedy trial, and that right must be defended vigorously. But until victims' speedy trial rights are respected, too, criminals and their lawyers will continue to abuse this important constitutional principle. Without blinking an eye, defense attorneys will drag out a victim's suffering for whatever strategic value they can get out of it; and unless we do something to ensure that criminal cases are resolved swiftly, victims like Debra Hagen and the system itself will continue to suffer.

You personally can help ensure that prosecutors don't shirk their responsibilities the way John Conte did in Debra's case. One way is to form citizens' groups and organize protests to openly shame inept district attorneys. Bill O'Reilly did this to great effect when Atlanta District Attorney Paul Howard allowed a baby-murderer to choose a sentence of tubal ligation for the crime of murdering her own infant. No jail time. No punishment. No sanction. She was sentenced to permanent birth control on the public's dime.

By applying intense pressure, the public learned a great deal about the district attorney's low opinion of the value of children's lives. This helps enormously at reelection time when people who care about certain types of crime (e.g., violence against women or children) can join together and use their strength in numbers to force the election of a better prosecutor.

Unfortunately, as effective as this is, it is one of the least-used strategies available to proponents of victims' rights. Why? In part, because most people have no idea who the elected prosecutor is in their jurisdiction. Law-abiding citizens don't like thinking about crime, so they don't focus on the race for district attorney and why it might matter to them in their everyday lives.

As a result, prosecutors are usually elected, based not on their qualifications or their commitment to crime prevention, but on the basis of factors like name recognition and whether they won any high-profile cases. Well, guess who provides much of the campaign financing to support the advertisements to boost a would-be DA's name recognition? You guessed it: defense attorneys. Victims don't really have lobbying power. Few people like to join a group whose common interest is that they suffered some horrible act of violence—people like to forget about pain. Organizations like rape-crisis centers and battered-women's programs which could help with political mobilization efforts, are too often afraid to criticize public officials, and many are run by partisan ideologues who promote classic liberal, antiprosecution ideas—so they're usually no help.

It's worse than bad. It's positively embarrassing that there aren't better organized groups of people out there working together to make sure the prosecutors being elected are the ones who are dedicated to protecting victims' rights and keeping our communities safe.

I know lots of you care about these issues, even if crime has never directly affected your life. That's why I'm calling on you to get involved right now. Talk to your friends and neighbors about who's running for district attorney. Help people understand why it's important to pick the right candidate. At election time, ask the candidates tough questions about how they plan to spend your tax dollars fighting crime and what specific steps they will take to ensure that victims' rights, such as the right to speedy justice, are protected. Then use your strength in numbers to lobby hard to make sure the best prosecutor wins.

If you and I don't get involved and stay involved in the political process that leads to the election of district attorneys, we'll get prosecutors like John Conte and Paul Howard every time. Our streets won't be safe. Injustice will prevail, and it will be our fault.

SEVEN

Manipulating the Media

IN CHAPTER 6, I INTRODUCED YOU TO A PARTICU-
larly objectionable character—the late James Kelly, a convicted
rapist who used newspaper accounts (among other tools) to help
fend off his incarceration for a decade. Unfortunately, Kelly isn't
the only bad guy who has used the media to manipulate the
court of public opinion and a court of law in an attempt to
evade justice. The same thing happened in the Scott Peterson,
Kobe Bryant, and Michael Jackson cases—circuses all, in which
the media trough was kept constantly filled with nonsense, much
of which was designed to distract the public and jurors from the

truth by getting them to focus on less important, though more entertaining, sideshows.

In high-profile criminal cases, defense by dog-and-pony-show tactics are virtually immune from sanctions. The defense can spin and dump lies into the court of public opinion and nothing can be done about it. But if the prosecutor did the same thing, or if the prosecutor told the *truth* about the evidence, the sanctions would be flying. Here's why. Judges can issue sanctions to prosecutors for causing too much prejudicial pretrial publicity. They can prevent prosecutors from using certain evidence at trial. Judges can even dismiss serious criminal charges as a way of punishing prosecutors for tainting the jury pool by revealing evidence prior to trial that shows how strong the government's case really is. But if the defense taints the jury pool, similar sanctions are not available. A judge can't punish the accused for the bad behavior of his lawyer by disallowing him a fair trial. Even if the defense makes completely false public statements about the victim, judges can't really do anything. This is why prosecutors usually say nothing while the defense can hold press conferences and say whatever they damn well please—truth and fairness to the victim be damned.

One more time: Prosecutors don't try to manipulate public opinion or even speak publicly about the truth because they don't want a judge to toss out their evidence or dismiss the charges, but the defense can speak publicly—and even lie—because there's virtually nothing the judge can do to punish them or otherwise put a stop to the nonsense. This is why during the Michael Jackson case, for example, the prosecutor said very little to the media while Jackson had no qualms about showing up in court one day wearing his pajamas and issuing public statements about his emotional suffering. Who can forget that scene? Jackson showed up late, hair all crooked, doing something that looked like the thorazine shuffle in a pair of PJs, and resembling a pathetic underfed psycho. Many people saw this as a thinly veiled attempt to win sympathy in court and from the general public.

I know it's strange to think a person would want that kind of sympathy—and it's possible he was truly under the weather—but come on, people about to drop dead from cancer at least put their pants on before they get to court. Most normal defendants wouldn't want to look like a crazy person, because it evokes the kind of prejudice that could push jurors toward a guilty verdict. Most defendants know the court-as-theater game well enough to know that when it comes to manipulating the jury, making yourself look like a nut isn't going to win you a lot of friends on the jury. But when you're Michael Jackson and there's a lot of evidence against you (a credible victim, admission you slept with children, police finding porn and booze rather than milk and cookies in your bedroom, and testimony that you've molested other boys in the past—I could go on), the jury might just give you a break if they think you're not so much dangerous as a hopelessly strange dude.

Funny thing is most people who know Jackson say he's anything but a nut. He's a slick businessman who knows exactly what he's doing.

Jackson was lucky that his whacky image—and his ability to use the media to saturate public consciousness with that image—allowed him to manipulate an awful lot of people to believe that even if he was guilty, he was not the "type" who should go to prison. So this irritated a lot of us, but tell me something: How is a prosecutor supposed to counter this stuff? How is the system supposed to nullify the effects of this performance? The answer is: It really can't. Which is why it just keeps happening. The best we can hope for, until someone changes the law, is that we will all be a little more cynical and suspicious when we see games being played. We can watch all these strategies with clearer vision if we keep in mind that defendants can do whatever they want—manipulate, spin, and lie—while the prosecutor is required to fight back with one hand tied behind his back. Keeping this imbalance in mind will help all of us judge high-profile cases more fairly.

Scott Peterson didn't play the nut card during his murder trial in 2004, but his lawyer used the media nonetheless in an attempt to manipulate the outcome. Knowing the media was covering every word, Attorney Mark Geragos repeatedly lobbed contrived bombshells onto the table at points during the trial when recent testimony had been especially damning to the defense. One week, it was a claim about a new DNA test that he said would identify the real killer. Another time it was a new witness who could prove Scott's innocence. Of course, none of this ever materialized into anything of significance. But Geragos knew exactly how to infect the news cycle by focusing people on the bombshells, rather than on the prosecution's mounting evidence. Not surprisingly, these bombshells were often dropped toward the end of the week to ensure that the entire weekend of cable news reporting and punditry would be devoted to analysis of the red herrings, rather than the unpleasant evidence of Peterson's guilt.

Peterson's lawyers had an extra advantage because we were all so riveted by the seeming mystery of it all, magnified by Peterson's icy-cold demeanor. How could a guy who killed his pregnant wife and unborn son at Christmastime be so cool? Wouldn't a guilty person be a withering mess? Being unsure makes us pay attention and being riveted by mystery is fine— but being riveted by lies is not. And we really shouldn't have been so glued to the tube given the overwhelming strength of the evidence. But our reluctance to believe the obvious helped some of us latch on to ridiculous theories about what happened. And even as we came to see with clarity how vicious Scott Peterson really was, we still couldn't look away because we then wanted to know *how* he did it and why. The how remains a big unknown today, though I have my theory. Laci was strangled to death as she was getting ready for bed the night before Scott reported her missing. Scott sneaked up behind his very pregnant wife after she took her shirt off (Laci's body was discovered dressed in the pants she'd been wearing the night before, and a maternity bra, but the shirt she'd had on was found in her laundry basket) and he grabbed her by the throat with both hands. As she struggled to breathe, Laci did what any of us would have done if we were being strangled from behind: She reached up with her right hand (she was right-handed) in an attempt to rip Scott's fingers off her neck. As Laci fought to breathe, she pulled hard, scraping her fingernails down the knuckles of Scott's left hand in a failed effort to release his grip. (Scott had cuts on the knuckles of three fingers of his left hand, cuts he said he got when he banged his hand on a toolbox in his truck, but tests showed there was no DNA or blood anywhere on the toolbox.)

You might not buy this theory—and that's okay—but it makes a hell of a lot more sense than some of the crazy things the defense was saying about a satanic cult kidnapping Laci in a brown van, and other such nonsense. Yet we heard those things every day during the Peterson trial, and we heard almost nothing about Scott's knuckles or the significance of Laci's half-dressed body.

Red-herring defense strategies are among the most serious problems in our legal system today. Why? Because the public thinks criminal trials are a search for the truth, and the unending stream of false revelations feeds right into this myth. Good, we think to ourselves, they're really digging deep into the facts and the evidence. We think we have our faith rewarded when, in fact, what's happening should make us cringe. The defense isn't searching for the truth, it's searching for a way to bury it. When the players assume that truth is irrelevant, then they're free to embrace any kind of distortion strategy—including dumping outright lies into the court of public opinion. This makes a mockery of any responsible definition of justice, but defense attorneys don't care.

One of the most vicious distortion tactics I've ever seen reared its ugly head in the Kobe Bryant case. Like when I hear the sound of fingers on a chalkboard, I was nearly debilitated when the defense asked in open court on October 9, 2003, whether the victim's vaginal injuries were consistent with her having "sex with three men in three days" around the time of the crime. It was obviously a distraction tactic, but would the general public figure it out? Would anyone even ask how the defense arrived at the number three? I did—and you won't believe the outrageous answer. First, they counted Bryant's sexual assault (hardly counts as sex). Then they counted a consensual interlude between the victim and her boyfriend two days before the assault (fair enough). Then they counted an incident that simply never occurred at all (three). What, you ask? They counted an imaginary incident? Yes. This alleged third incident grew out of the discovery of unidentified microscopic sperm cells that did not match Bryant's DNA. The defense theory was that the sperm were deposited when the victim had sex with someone after she left the hotel, and before she got home.

The obvious absurdity of this claim should have prevented anyone with a brain from repeating it as if true. But what can I say? A lot of people were grasping onto anything to help their beloved Kobe Bryant. I'm not saying it's impossible for anyone ever to have consensual sex during the drive home after being raped. But there was absolutely no evidence that such an event happened in the Bryant case, and unidentified DNA proved nothing on this issue. Let me tell you why.

The mystery DNA consisted of only dead sperm cells with no tails. A whopping total of four dead tailless sperm from the mystery man were found inside the victim's body. Better yet, there was no semen! Given that one ejaculation produces millions and millions of sperm, *and* that they need a ride to get out of the body (that's what semen is for), *and* that they live for up to five days (tails fall off when they die), the old and dead nature of the sperm, plus the fact that only four were found in the victim's body, is indisputable evidence that there was no post-rape sex. District attorney Mark Hurlbert told me the "mystery" DNA found on the victim was all of the same old and dead quality, from the same person—most likely the victim's boyfriend—and most certainly from an encounter weeks earlier. But this didn't inhibit a defense expert named Dr. Elizabeth Johnson from stating under oath "to a reasonable degree of scientific certainty," that the dead sperm evidence was nevertheless "consistent with" the victim having sex after Bryant's assault and before she went to the hospital early the next day. Or, as Bryant's lawyer put it, "having sex with three men in three days."

Saying the victim had sex with three men in three days worked wonders to distract the public from paying any attention to all the damning evidence about Bryant's behavior that had been revealed in court earlier that same day. The allegations were pretty gruesome—that Bryant grabbed the victim by the neck, bent her over a chair, raped her from behind with such force and friction her genital area tore and started bleeding. (The injury had nothing to do with Bryant's size, another racist myth bandied about during the case.) The victim's blood was found on the underside of Bryant's T-shirt, and he reportedly admonished her not to tell anyone what happened before sending her away like a piece of trash. The defense needed more than a red herring to distract the public's attention away from this evidence, and they didn't have it, so they created it out of whole cloth. The sex-with-three-men-in-three-days announcement was far more than a red herring, it was a neon scarlet killer whale, injected into the court of public opinion by Bryant's lawyer, Pamela Mackey, irrespective of the truth. Why would she do this? No doubt because it had all the salacious qualities that would make a sex-crazed public sit up and take notice, thus ignoring the horrifying evidence. And it was exactly the type of evidence the hungry Bryant–fan club was aching for; the kind of information they could latch on to that would help them feel better about rooting for a superstar athlete accused of a brutal crime.

Few people cared that an innocent crime victim who had already suffered enough was being harmed for sport. The public paid almost no attention to the gruesome testimony about Bryant's conduct. Do you think the timing of the statement was coincidental? I don't.

For months thereafter, the mainstream news media and almost every pundit on the planet—myself and a couple of others excluded—repeated the lie. When I was asked about it, I would take a deep breath and cite the relevant allegations: "Bryant bent her over a chair, raped her from behind, and tore her genital area, leaving her blood on his T-shirt."

The host would brush that statement off and say something like, "Well, okay, Wendy, that's all well and good, but let's talk about the sex-with-three-men-in-three-days issue."

Once again, I'd take a deep breath, roll my eyes, and say, "He bent her over a chair . . ." And so on, and so on. I knew the game—and I wasn't playing.

When the victim's lawyer tried to correct the lie by issuing a statement dismissing the claim as false, the judge, Terry Ruckriegle, hauled him into court and threatened him with contempt for violating the gag order. At the same time, Ruckriegle never punished Pamela Mackey for lying about the victim's sexual conduct—or for any of the other outrageous things Mackey did, like "accidentally" identifying the victim by name over and over again in open court. Calling the victim by her real name wouldn't be such a big deal if she hadn't repeatedly been threatened with death by Bryant sycophants and sicko fans. Judge Ruckriegle didn't seem to care very much about the victim's safety or Mackey's lies. He should have held Mackey in contempt or filed ethical charges against her.

Let's be clear about this: The truth was contemptuous, but the lies were perfectly okay. Judge Ruckriegle should feel terrible for what he did. No judge should allow an innocent victim to be needlessly harmed by such an outrageous defense strategy, but don't hold your breath waiting for an apology.

Kobe Bryant is a popular guy and an excellent athlete—no doubt worth a fortune to the Lakers. These things matter a lot in our understanding of why so few people protested the unfair things that happened in that case. In turn, these things also explain why the case was dismissed. It wasn't because of great lawyering, as some argued. Any idiot can make up lies. But for a price, Mackey made sure the Lakers held on to their star shooting guard, and that was all that mattered.

At least it's over now and all is well with the world, right? Not exactly. Criminals everywhere (along with their lawyers) learned a few lessons from Bryant's high-priced tricksters. Thanks to the defense-at-any-cost nonsense in Bryant's case, it seems a safe bet that this sort of vile lawyering will be coming soon to a courthouse near you. Nice.

For my part, I'm not waiting until the next circus to take action. I'm fighting right now for new laws that explicitly authorize victims and their lawyers to speak publicly—without threat of contempt—whenever a false statement is made about a victim. And we need laws that will immediately strip lawyers of their licenses to practice law, forever, if they make public statements that are false and which expose victims to an increased risk of serious violence during a criminal case.

We also need more education about the deceptive things defense attorneys get away with in the name of winning. Jurors in the real court—and in the court of public opinion—have to start assessing the information they receive from defense sources, both inside the courtroom and out, with an appropriate level of skepticism. Think about all the things we've learned to be skeptical about—like whether the jelly people paid for a study that "proves" marshmallow fluff is bad for kids because they want to be peanut butter's exclusive sandwich partner. Let's learn to be skeptical of well-timed media bombshells in criminal cases, too.

And we need the media to do a better job writing about criminal cases. Journalism is supposed to be about getting at the truth. But in court, winning is the only goal, especially for the defense. Given this reality, the media should take extra care not simply to report what the defense says, and then let the other side respond by saying that it's not true. This isn't fair because the defense has far more freedom than the prosecution has, not only to make public statements but also to misstate the truth.

But it is exactly what happened in the Kobe Bryant case. The media wrote that the defense claimed the victim had "sex with three men in three days"—and that the victim's lawyer said it wasn't true. Reporters who later found out the truth told me they thought this was fair because both sides had their say. But if what the defense says is either highly misleading, or—as in Bryant's case—flat-out false, the media should not simply print what is said in court and feel okay about it, so long as they give the victim a chance to say not true. It just isn't fair to create the appearance that both sides' positions have equal weight, especially when the lie is so salacious and so much is at stake for a real victim.

Defense attorneys often complain about grand jury leaks, as well they should. It's patently unfair when the government secretly slips information to the media at a point in the process when the accused has little hope of defending himself. But let's be honest. While prosecutors leak, defense attorneys gush. And though grand jury leaks are bad, lies are worse. At least the grand jury testimony has some credibility. It's given under oath in a formal judicial proceeding and prosecutors can face ethical and other sanctions if they intentionally present false evidence to a grand jury. I would never claim that all grand jury testimony is truthful, but journalists can take some comfort in publishing the information because lies under oath can be prosecuted as felonies, which helps to deter people from making false statements. But statements by defense counsel in court aren't under oath and aren't subject to any preliminary scrutiny for truthfulness or reliability, which means the media's policy of publishing information based solely on the fact that the lawyer for the accused said it in court is a policy that subverts journalistic standards. That Mackey's comment was supported by the claims set forth in an "expert" affidavit makes no difference. Sadly, there are no rules that effectively prohibit hired guns for the defense from filing affidavits or testifying under oath that up is down and black is white.

And finally, in every case when the media realizes it got snookered into parroting a harmful lie about a victim that has been floated by the defense, it has to issue a correction, and it has to apologize for dragging an innocent person's reputation through the mud.

The misuse of media as a tool by which false information is dumped into the court of public opinion in criminal cases is way out of control. But we can all do something about it by checking facts ourselves, using the internet and blog sites to talk with others about the truth, writing letters to the editor when the media gets it wrong and simply being skeptical consumers of news. The longer we wait, the greater the chance public cynicism about the criminal justice system will start to infect the fourth estate. Call me a doomsayer, but these days I don't think the press needs society to have any extra reasons to be suspicious about how they do their job.

Eight

Picking Dumb Jurors

Much of what we've been talking about in re-
cent chapters is what I call distortion tactics. There's no polite
way to say what's coming next, so I'll just plunge ahead: Distortion tactics work particularly well when the jury's collective IQ
hovers somewhere around dumb as a rock.

Only the dimmest of jurors buy into the kinds of crazy an-
tics that are designed to divert their attention away from the real
and important evidence. So it should come as no surprise to you
that in general, defense attorneys try their damndest to identify
and seat all the dopes they can get their hands on during the
jury selection process. Yes, there are exceptions to this rule. By

and large, however, dummies are good for an unscrupulous defense attorney who needs desperately to persuade someone to look away from the evidence, ignore common sense, and vote not guilty because of a ridiculous claim that has no basis in reality. Sure, sometimes even smart jurors act like idiots, but not too many can be tricked into an outright acquittal of a clearly guilty criminal. The defense knows that one nitwit is all it takes. So the hunt for nitwits is usually the name of the game when it comes to jury selection.

This is insulting—to me, to you, and to our justice system. And yet nobody is doing anything about it.

Ever since the O. J. verdict in 1995, dumb-juror syndrome has been on the rise. Lawyers everywhere learned about the power of stupid, and jury consultants developed psychological sonar to find these types of people in the sea of citizens who show up for jury duty. Is it any wonder that today we see so many acquittals in the face of overwhelming evidence?

Even worse, some people actually try to get selected for certain types of cases, especially high-profile trials, so they can screw things up on purpose. Jurors can lack basic reasoning skills but be smart enough to know that there might be fame and fortune ahead if they get picked for a big case. Whether the motivation is to sell a book, punish the police, or just enjoy fifteen minutes of fame, the jury system is awash in a flood of brainless and selfish morons—citizens who you would think care at least a little bit about the integrity of the system. After all, they showed up for jury duty, which is more than I can say for a lot of citizens. But showing up is no guarantee of good character. Sorry if this sounds harsh, but it has to be said because it's a real problem.

And as if having a lot of numbskulls meting out—or thwarting—justice isn't bad enough, there's mounting evidence of a problem that I call lying-juror syndrome.

During a murder trial in Boston in 2004, it was uncovered during deliberations that five out of twelve jurors lied under oath on questionnaires about whether they had ever been convicted of a crime. Not one, or two, but five jurors had lied to the criminal justice system about being convicted criminals, even though the questionnaire itself warns jurors that lying on the form is a crime.

Despite significant public outrage about the case, none of the jurors was prosecuted. With such a namby-pamby prosecutorial response, there's no reason to believe that this kind of nonsense won't continue.

I'm not suggesting than anyone convicted of a crime can never sit on a jury. Some of the best jurors are people with street smarts, who know more than the average Joe about how the bad guys do business. But can't we all agree that people who commit perjury on their jury forms might not be the pick of the litter when it comes to building public confidence in the decision-making process.

Even stranger than the fact that nothing happened to the lying jurors is that Willie Davis, the lawyer for the defendant whose case was being judged by these jurors, had the audacity to file a motion with the court complaining that the prosecution should be sanctioned for violating the jurors' privacy rights when a search was conducted of the criminal record database to determine whether the jurors had been truthful in claiming under oath that they had no rap sheet. Think about this: He argued that convicted criminals should have such powerful privacy rights in their rap sheets that law enforcement officials should be punished for looking at the jurors' criminal records to determine whether they committed perjury.

This is what we've come to. As you've read throughout this book, criminals lie, jurors lie, defense attorneys lie, and nothing happens; but if the prosecutor tries to do something about jurors' committing perjury, he should get in trouble for invading their privacy. What's that saying about the nuts running the asylum?

We also have jurors who simply can't focus on the evidence at hand because they get the hots for the lawyers themselves. This was the syndrome du jour during the William Kennedy Smith rape trial, when one idiot went ga-ga for Smith's lawyer, Roy Black. She voted not guilty and then married the guy after the case was over. All I can say is, too bad the assistant district attorney didn't look like Pamela Anderson. If these are the things that drive jurors' decisions, maybe a sex-crazed male juror would have voted guilty in the hope of getting a date with the prosecutor. At least there would have been balance to the craziness.

Then there's the celebrity factor. Whatever else jurors suffer from in general—whether an affinity for crime, hormonal overloads, or some other defect—there is no rational explanation for the not-guilty verdict in the Michael Jackson case except that in addition to being dumb, jurors can't think straight when the accused is famous. This might be called the stupid-and-celebrity-crazed-juror syndrome. It's embarrassing, but true: If you are a beloved, famous somebody in this country and you commit a crime, you'll probably never see a day behind bars—assuming, of course, that your defense team picks enough jurors who are so hopelessly starstruck that they're literally unable to look at and listen to the evidence because they're only thinking about touching your hand or begging for an autograph.

This is apparently what happened with the prosecution of Michael Jackson. Jackson simply was too popular, and some might say too pathetic, to convict. We probably shouldn't overlook the fact that he put the struggling town of Santa Maria, California, on the map, too. Perhaps it was wishful thinking to expect that they would ever send their only claim to fame to prison.

The fact that the jurors in the Jackson case got it so badly wrong—on the world stage and so soon after the O. J. Simpson debacle—makes the loss a colossal, compounded embarrassment for all Americans. As I noted in the introduction, we like to brag to other countries that we have the best system on the planet. But then, in a couple of high-profile cases where the evidence of guilt is overwhelming, we show our true colors, and they are not pretty.

The Simpson verdict was painful enough, but the Jackson verdict—yeesh! Excuse me, but what did the nitwits think Jackson was doing with the jar of Vaseline next to the porn on the night table next to the bed where—according to one of Jackson's own witnesses—the pedo-perp boasted about sleeping with one little boy 365 times? This is not rocket science.

Maybe we can take a little comfort from the fact that a few jurors in the Jackson case had an after-the-fact epiphany about how wrong they had been. They described not just pressure but outright bullying by other jurors to render a not-guilty verdict.

One said jurors were told they would be removed from the case if they did not vote to acquit. Another said he was lied to by jurors, who told him the law required them to vote not guilty if they had even a tiny bit of doubt. This assertion about doubt is not true. Jurors can and should find a defendant guilty even if they have doubt—as long as the doubt is not "unreasonable." The bully jurors and the ones who lied about the definition of reasonable doubt should be sought out and punished.

When jurors are idiots, they can't judge witnesses fairly, because they don't understand that they have to rise above their own cloudy vision of the world in order to be truly fair. This is hard for all of us to do, but when we accept the responsibility to sit in judgment as jurors, we have to be mindful of our own limitations. This is not something most jurors think about because, in most states, jurors are not even admonished to be fair to witnesses and victims. The law typically only requires that judges instruct jurors not to be biased toward "either party." Since victims and witnesses are not "parties" to the criminal case, jurors are effectively told they can be biased against them.

Great. No wonder the jurors were so quick to blame the Jackson victim's mother for their decision to acquit the creep. She may well have been a troubled soul, but almost every scandalous thing we heard about her was completely irrelevant. The jurors clearly did not understand this, given that one of them remarked after the verdict that she had voted not guilty, in part, because she didn't like the victim's mother. This woman literally said, "What kind of mother would let her son sleep at Michael Jackson's house?"

Two troubling thoughts come to mind. First, this particular

juror obviously discounted Jackson's responsibility for the crime, not based on the evidence but because of her own negative feelings about the victim's mother. I let this woman have it when I did commentary on TV regarding her explanation for the verdict. Why didn't she have the basic common sense to know that even if the victim's mother laid her own son out naked on Jackson's bed and invited Jackson to pounce, the twisted pop star still had absolutely no right to touch that child? If nothing the mother did could excuse Jackson, then the jurors had no business relying on how they felt about the mother to reach their not-guilty verdict. Shame on every member of the jury that failed to understand this!

The second troubling thought is that this particular juror thought the victim's mother was a bad parent for letting her son sleep at Jackson's house. What's the obvious inference? Jackson is dangerous to young boys. So how in God's name did this juror vote not guilty if she thought the guy was so damn dangerous?

The sad fact is that in jurisdictions around the country where common sense is in limited supply, the jury system is in deep trouble—and no one is doing anything about it. No, this is not a comment on wealth, race, or any other easy sorting mechanism. One thing I know for sure, from my years in the courtroom, is that people in all types of communities, wealthy or poor, educated or not, can lack basic logic skills. For example, I had a case in which a teacher-juror voted to acquit on one of several charges in a child-rape case because he thought the victim learned how to lie about being raped after the first couple of assaults. An educated juror, yes, but clearly an idiot. This is not a comment on the type of citizen who lives in that geographic area. Indeed, it was a jury from this same region—around Cambridge, Massachusetts—that had tons of common sense as evidenced by their capacity to convict Louise Woodward of murder in 1997 for the brutal shaking and beating death of baby Matthew Eappen. This high-profile case, known as the Nanny Trial, was dominated by scientific blather from one defense expert after the next. The multisyllabic babble from reputable academic experts—about how the child could have died from a minor bump on the head that slowly grew over time until one day the minor bump exploded and the baby died—went on for days, and days. It felt like a dense scientific fog was settling in to suffocate the truth in the courtroom.

But the stark backdrop against which this fog rolled in was that no child in the history of mankind had ever died in the way that the defense experts said this baby died. The jury smartly believed the medical professionals who tried to save Matty Eappen's life, the experts who were not paid a fortune for their testimony and who testified that the baby had all the earmarks of having been shaken violently and slammed against a hard surface: retinal bleeding, unique perimacular (accordion-like) folds in his eyes and a 2½-inch-long skull fracture.

The jury kept hold of their common sense despite the dog-and-pony show and found Woodward guilty of murder. Woodward's lawyer, Barry Sheck, complained after the guilty verdict that the jury wasn't smart enough to understand the complicated scientific evidence—the fog, as it were. I laughed when I heard this. "Barry's just a sore loser," I said on one television program. "The truth is, he tried but couldn't find enough dopes to stuff on a jury in Cambridge, Massachusetts."

But this wasn't quite right. You can find dumb jurors everywhere. Or, stated differently, you can wind up with dumb or deranged jurors no matter where the case is tried because we rarely ask jurors enough basic questions to know whether or not they are even competent to serve.

A couple of years ago, one of my students said she'd recently been a juror in a case where she was particularly interested in the opinion of a relatively silent juror, who—my student had concluded—must be the smartest one among them because he seemed the most pensive, intent on keeping his thoughts to himself while others droned on annoyingly about mundane topics. She became increasingly irritated by the talkative jurors who seemed unable to process information logically. Eventually, she sought out the quiet guy's opinion, approaching him directly to ask a question about the evidence. He didn't reply—not because he was particularly thoughtful, but because he had no idea what she was asking him. He didn't speak a word of English. So the guy not only had no idea what she was asking him, he hadn't understood what any of the witnesses had said when they took the stand. This juror had the power to determine whether a person was guilty of a crime—the biggest responsibility that our society asks us to take on as citizens—and he didn't speak the language!

We clearly need new laws that mandate juror screening to eliminate those who are unwilling to listen or incapable of understanding the evidence. For the results of jury trials to be worthy of the public's respect, we need jurors to bring at least a baseline of intelligence and common sense to the process. And we need new laws to mandate that jurors be instructed not to be biased against victims and witnesses, as well as the parties to the case.

We also need swift and strong punishment for jurors who lie on their questionnaires. The minute the public hears about a prosecution of a juror for lying, the news will spread like wildfire, and all potential future jurors will get the message: Jury duty is serious business.

This country has a very generous Bill of Rights for accused criminals, but there's no such thing as a constitutional right to select only dumb jurors. New laws will take a lot of work because defense attorneys count on jurors having weak IQs. They're not about to let the public undermine their scoresheet without a fight. But that's okay, it's a worthy battle.

Remember (Wendy) Murphy's Law. This will only continue if we let it and there is only one choice. We can't develop a pill to make every citizen juror at least minimally competent, so we have to work together to keep the problem jurors away from the courthouses. I've suggested a few ways we can get this done but I'm sure you have ideas of your own. The most important thing is that we get started—right now.

NINE

Exploiting Victims' Fears

THE MEANEST TRICK THAT HURTS ALL VICTIMS—AND impairs the ability of the justice system to protect us from harm—arises when defense lawyers negotiate bargain-basement plea deals or otherwise gain strategic advantages by exploiting a victim's fears and suffering. The thing I despise the most is when defense attorneys in child-abuse cases invoke the argument that good parents always accept plea bargains in order to protect their child from the trauma of testifying.

It's a very appealing argument. Who wouldn't want to protect a child victim from additional suffering? The problem is it can lead to outright dismissals of serious criminal charges.

Do you think parents, even great ones, aren't vulnerable to this kind of pressure? Of course they are. In most cases, they're encountering something new and horrifying and scary, and they want to protect their child. When someone tells them what a good parent does in such a situation, they're very often open to any suggestion that will make the whole horrible thing go away.

It's terribly sad that the harsh realities of the justice system—made harsh in large part by unrestrained defense tactics—have become a powerful weapon in the game of plea bargaining. But it's going on every single day in every corner of the country. It's bad enough that criminals get to negotiate discounts by doing things like refusing to reveal their HIV status unless the victim agrees to a sentence of probation. And who can forget the disgusting, bottom-feeding lawyers for David Westerfield—the man convicted in 2002 of murdering little seven-year-old Danielle Van Dam—who tried to negotiate what will go down in history as the most outrageous of attempted plea deals. Before Danielle's body was found, attorneys Steven Feldman and Robert Boyce tried to score a deal for Westerfield by offering to reveal Danielle's location in exchange for the prosecution's dropping its plan to seek the death penalty.

The lawyers who propose these types of negotiations should go to prison.

Thankfully, Danielle's body was uncovered before the deal was made—but think about this: Should a child murderer get a discount because the victim's parents are desperate to find the remains of their little girl? Is there a more inhumane way to run a legal system? Westerfield's lawyers will never rid themselves of the shame they deserve for even trying to broker such a deal. Both men will fail the pillows-and-mirror test for the rest of their lives—meaning, they won't sleep well and won't easily be able to look at themselves, without feeling sick. This is as it should be, because nobody who has the capacity to treat such a serious matter like a swap meet deserves peace of mind.

Trading on information is one thing. Scaring kids away from justice is equally wrong. But this is exactly what happened when Rhode Island elementary-school principal, church volunteer, and Little League coach John W. Card admitted in court to molesting a child repeatedly over a period of several years. He had been charged with committing forty-eight sex crimes against a male student, including rape. Under a plea bargain with the attorney general's office, Card pleaded guilty to only one count of second-degree child molestation and was set free on a suspended sentence. The rationale for this ridiculously lenient sentence was that the victim did not want to testify at trial. Not surprisingly, Card waited until the eve of trial to plead guilty—when his victim's fears and anxieties were at their peak—before using the intimidating nature of the system to force the prosecution to hand him a bargain-basement sentence.

A similar save-the-child theme was in the air when John Andrews, the attorney for child rapist and rampant Massachusetts pedophile Christopher Reardon, claimed in 2002 that his client was pleading guilty on the eve of trial to "spare the children" the pain of testifying. Reardon, a church and community volunteer, had been indicted on 150 counts of sexual abuse and related crimes against nearly twenty children. A few weeks before trial, the victims' parents submitted affidavits explaining that their children were ready to testify but would be severely traumatized if their testimony were subjected to televised coverage. The defense objected. When the parents' efforts to keep the TV cameras out failed, Reardon agreed to plead guilty on the eve of trial—but only after the prosecution offered to reduce the number of charges by half to approximately seventy-five.

If Reardon and Attorney Andrews really wanted to spare the children, they wouldn't have objected to the parents' request to keep cameras out. And if Reardon really wanted to spare the children, the jerk certainly could have pled guilty long before the eve of trial. Keep in mind that these kids were teenagers at the time of trial—a difficult, busy, and turbulent phase of life. Reardon and his lawyer made these kids suffer needlessly, every day, thinking about how the grotesque things Reardon did to them would soon be televised for all their friends to see, in lurid detail.

Nobody did anything to stop the defense from exploiting the victims and their anxieties to get the most value in their plea-bargain negotiations. Shameful, all around.

Even those who sincerely have the victim's best interest at heart sometimes give away the store on tough punishments because they think it's important to protect children from testifying. Texas Judge G. Timothy Boswell sentenced forty-six-year-old police officer Richard Wilson to probation as part of a plea bargain after Wilson was charged with raping or molesting three girls and one boy, aged eleven to fifteen. The prosecutor, Marcus Taylor, went along with the plea bargain, claiming that a therapist thought it was not in the best interest of one of the victims to testify. This was a curious excuse, given that the victims had testified at an earlier trial that ended in a mistrial after one of the victims recanted her testimony. (By the way, recantations are almost always false.) If it was in the kids' best interest to testify at the first trial when they were even younger, how did it become not in their best interest at the second trial?

If a child in any criminal trial is legitimately too traumatized to testify but has given statements in an earlier trial or other legal proceeding, the judge should *not* allow a plea bargain, but instead should permit the prosecutor to substitute for the child's live testimony a transcript of what the child said at that earlier proceeding. This is permissible in some states as long as the defense has had a prior opportunity to conduct cross-examination. In many states, a transcript of the statements can come into evidence without the child's taking the stand if the prosecutor can prove that the defendant's behavior caused the child to become so terrified that he became psychologically unavailable to testify. This so-called forfeiture-by-wrongdoing rule is a great idea—not used nearly enough by prosecutors. It allows all kinds of evidence to be used against the accused at trial, even if it would otherwise violate his constitutional rights, because a perpetrator forfeits his constitutional rights if he causes a victim or a witness to become too afraid to take the stand.

In many cases, a prosecutor can prove his case without calling the child to the stand. Sometimes evidence such as medical records and statements the child made to a doctor or parent establish that a crime occurred. And lots of times the perpetrator admits to at least some aspects of the crime. These statements are almost always admissible. The best prosecutors usually try to piece together a case without forcing the child to take the stand. The crummy ones just make deals on the backs of kids.

If a case truly cannot be won without the child, then the child should be compelled to testify, except in rare cases and only after a child psychologist examines the child to assess the likelihood of serious harm. Age, alone, should never be the reason for a deal. If prosecutors have to spend time and money on an expert, chances are good that they will think twice about giving a predator a deal unless the well-being of a child is truly at stake. While it is undoubtedly true that the well-being of a young victim is more important than justice, it is also true that the well-being of a child is not usually at risk when save-the-child plea bargains are struck.

Noted researcher Gail Goodman, a professor of psychology at the University of California at Davis, studied the well-being of twenty-seven child victims who testified in sexual-abuse cases. She found that many showed emotional improvement after testifying. In a similar group of children who were not required to testify, Goodman interviewed the victims as adults and found that many were expressing regret, saying things like "I wish I could have testified." These data suggest that while the value of confronting an abuser in court may not appear clear to a child at the time of their testimony, there is obviously a psychological benefit and a feeling of empowerment for many children in simply participating in the trial. Consider, for example, an eight-year-old client of mine who was repeatedly sexually assaulted by a babysitter. At first, his parents didn't want him to testify. They'd been told it would be a terrible experience and they didn't want to put their son through it. But when the time came for trial, the child took the stand and testified about what had been done to him. The jury found the perpetrator not guilty, in part because the child couldn't remember all the details with precision. No child ever does. It didn't matter much to the little boy. He was proud of himself. Years later his mother told me he described his experience like this: "I was sitting in the big chair next to the judge. I felt scared and I could see the bad guy staring at me, so I looked over at the American flag. There was a gold eagle on the top, so I kept my focus on the eagle. I remember thinking that I kind of felt like an eagle—strong and proud of myself for telling the truth about what happened." True, these are benefits that a child might not understand until adulthood. Nevertheless, the adults around them are duty bound to consider these complexities before giving away the store, thereby letting a dangerous predator walk free.

Even if a child might be traumatized by the experience of testifying, it is important to remember that all kids are placed at greater risk of harm when a dangerous predator is inadequately punished. The strong arm of the government often forces reluctant witnesses to testify in serious criminal proceedings, simply because the system cannot function otherwise. This forceful approach sends an appropriately strong message about society's intolerance for serious violence. When isn't the rape or sodomy of a child *serious* violence?

And how bad will the trial be for the child? Consider this. Defense attorneys can't get away with harshly attacking a young victim's credibility. There's too great a risk the jury won't like it and will hold it against the defendant. I've never seen a defense attorney harshly question a child.

It's time to stop disrespecting kids in the name of protection; we need prosecutors and judges with spines. We need new laws—state constitutional amendments if necessary—to make the criminal justice system more user-friendly for young victims.

And we need more resources earmarked for prosecutors and police to do a better job investigating and prosecuting witness intimidation and obstruction-of-justice charges against anyone who attempts to keep a child off the stand by bribing, coercing, or scaring a victim or a victim's parents.

Finally, all prosecutors should immediately announce to the public the adoption of a no drop/no deal policy in child-abuse cases. Perpetrators will be less inclined to scare kids when they realize it won't do them any good. And who knows, given that certain predators pick on kids because they know they stand a good chance of scaring their victims into silence, no drop/no deal policies may well discourage them from choosing children as their victims.

Yes, the cost of a no drop/no deal policy includes the possibility that a few children will be negatively affected during criminal trials. But remember: Testifying in court doesn't necessarily traumatize children; and it is often psychologically beneficial. And at the end of the day, forcing child victims to testify will better protect all our precious children from hideous abuses.

We owe this aggressive approach to kids because we've never really done right by our most vulnerable citizens. We had laws on the books in this country to protect animals from abuse before we had laws to protect children from abuse. How can this be true, you wonder? I'm sure it's because a couple of hundred years ago, we literally thought animals were more valuable than kids. Shocking, I know—and we've certainly improved since then—but we bear the legacy of that ugliness in our legal system to this very day, every time we give out discounts to child predators. One researcher found that on average, a homicide against a child receives one-fourth the punishment that the same offense would carry if committed against an adult. This is unacceptable, and it's time to put to rest the offensive idea that crimes against defenseless citizens are easy to get away with because the value of children's lives is cheap.

Let's get really tough on child abuse for a change. And let's get this done soon. Children are usually very good witnesses because they're not very good liars. The pedophiles know this, which is why they are far more frightened of a child taking the stand than the child is afraid of testifying. The perpetrators are waiting for us to make the wrong decision. Remember (Wendy) Murphy's Law? They can't get away with it if we don't let them.

What's your choice?

TEN

Using the Cross-Fingerpointing Maneuver

ONE OF THE MOST FRUSTRATING SITUATIONS EN-
countered by law enforcement is when they know for certain
that two people were present at the scene of a crime but only one
of them is guilty—and neither of them is talking. Usually, this
happens when the guilty party persuades the innocent one that
if they infect the crime scene with enough evidence to lead police to believe either one of them could be guilty, and if they
stick together like glue, neither one can be prosecuted.

I call this the cross-fingerpointing trick, because each suspect has the potential to point the finger of blame at the other.
As long as they didn't commit the crime together, which would

make the case prosecutable under a conspiracy or joint-venture theory, the case against the real killer is essentially unprosecutable because the innocent buddy agrees to serve as the real killer's built-in reasonable doubt.

The defense bar loves this trick. And they have a sarcastic saying that sums up this tactic, which I think you should be aware of: Nobody talks, everybody walks. Remember: These are defense attorneys talking—often public defenders—which means we're talking about your tax dollars at work.

In gang-violence cases, where cops can pressure the suspects individually to get someone to roll, the nobody-talks maneuver doesn't usually work for long. But it works quite well when the two suspects are family members who live together because police can't easily gain sufficient enough access to either one, alone, to get at the truth. They can try by asking for separate interviews but if the suspects refuse, police will have a hard time persuading one or the other to cooperate.

In Florida, law enforcement officials have been frustrated in their efforts to solve the 1997 disappearance and possible murder of "baby Sabrina." Sabrina's parents, Steve and Marlene Aisenberg, have denied any involvement but have not been cleared; and no charges have been filed against either one of them. One explanation is that police believe one of them is responsible, but if they pursue charges against the mother, she can point the finger at the father, and vice versa.

Similarly, in Connecticut, the murder of Martha Moxley in 1975 went unsolved for two decades, in part because even though police knew that one of the two Skakel brothers (celebrated Kennedy-related neighbors of the victim) was most likely responsible for Moxley's death, they could not be certain that a trial against either one would be successful, because each brother could credibly demonstrate reasonable doubt by implicating the other. Tommy Skakel was the last person seen with Moxley, but Michael Skakel was eventually tried and convicted in 2002, after making enough damning statements about his involvement to tip the scales firmly in favor of prosecution. Unexpectedly— and to the credit of either the Skakel family, who found the idea unconscionable, or his attorney, Mickey Sherman—Michael did not falsely point the finger at his brother, Tommy, during trial.

In a more recent example of a possible cross-fingerpointing problem, from Colorado, the parents of baby Jason Midyette have been under the umbrella of suspicion for more than a year after their baby became seriously injured and died in March 2006. When medical professionals asked what happened, the parents hired criminal defense lawyers and clammed up. Obviously law enforcement is suspicious, but if the parents are the only potential suspects in a particular case because nobody else had ongoing access to the baby, how can police ever prove which one did what?

The most famous cross-fingerpointing case, interestingly enough coming out of the same jurisdiction as the Midyette case (Boulder, Colorado), is surely that of JonBenet Ramsey, the six-year-old little girl who was murdered and sexually assaulted in her own home on Christmas night 1996. Many people believe that one of the parents, John or Patsy, killed JonBenet; and if this is true, the cross-fingerpointing trick, more than any of the nonsense about intruders, corruption, and dim-witted prosecutors, explains why neither parent was ever charged with a crime.

We all know that neither John nor Patsy has been charged with or found guilty of any wrongdoing. But let's assume hypothetically for the moment that John Ramsey, alone, killed his daughter. One way for him to avoid being charged and to ensure Patsy's silence would be to make sure the evidence suggested that Patsy was involved, too. If he instructed Patsy to write the ransom note and forced her to help with the cover-up, John could easily demonstrate reasonable doubt as to his guilt at trial by implying that Patsy was the real killer.

As the evidence developed in the Ramsey case, the focus on the parents as suspects intensified, but things did not become clearer as to which parent might have done what to the child.

On the one hand, *Vanity Fair* published a story that said Patsy gave inconsistent statements about whether she found the ransom note before or after she noticed JonBenet's missing from her bed. And former detective Steve Thomas wrote a book opining that Patsy Ramsey killed JonBenet because she was enraged about the child's bed-wetting.

On the other hand, in August 2000, investigators told John Ramsey when they questioned him in his lawyer's office that black wool sweater fibers that matched one of John Ramsey's sweaters were found in the crotch area of the size twelve (much too large for a six-year-old), not previously worn underpants the child was wearing when her body was found. Ramsey did not answer the question directly. In fact, Ramsey and his lawyer, Lin Wood, did what lawyers do when investigators ask tough questions that back the suspect into a corner: They filibustered and used profanity. Ramsey said, "That's bullshit," and Wood fulminated about how he couldn't possibly answer the question without seeing the forensic report. Suffice it to say that if they had a legitimate explanation at the time for such damning evidence, there would have been no yelling and no blather. If they have one now, I wish they would call me and tell me about it.

Despite the fiber evidence, if police did believe John killed JonBenet, Patsy's seeming involvement in aspects of the crime would continue to frustrate prosecution efforts because of the very real risk that John could easily prevail at trial by pointing the finger at Patsy. Indeed, Patsy's red sweater fibers were found at the crime scene too; on duct tape that covered the child's mouth and intertwined in the ligature around the child's neck.

Interestingly, one of the Ramseys' lawyers is now also a lawyer for one of the Midyette parents. And maybe not surprisingly, in both cases, the parents spoke with lawyers and clammed up in the immediate aftermath of the crime. The Ramseys claim they cooperated, but the truth is their lawyer told the police soon after JonBenet's body was discovered that the Ramseys were represented by criminal-defense attorneys and would not be going to the police station, as requested, for formal and separate interviews.

The cross-fingerpointing trick in the Ramsey case is especially effective because the public is uncomfortable accepting the idea that people who look so nice on the outside can be dastardly on the inside. This feel-good bias makes it harder to conceptualize that a parent could commit a horrific crime against his or her own child or that an innocent parent could possibly want to help the killer-parent avoid prosecution. Even if the prosecutors felt confident about the evidence, they had to worry about what jurors would think—and as an ethical matter, they couldn't proceed unless they believed they could persuade a jury about one parent's guilt beyond a reasonable doubt.

After Patsy died of cancer in 2006, speculation was rampant that her death might lead to a break in the case. But in a cross-fingerpointing situation, death of one suspect changes nothing. The prosecutor still has to deal with the very real problem that the surviving suspect can raise reasonable doubt by pointing at the dead suspect. In a way it's even better for the survivor because if the dead suspect is the innocent one, it's harder for a prosecutor to prove innocence from the grave.

To deal with this intensely frustrating dirty trick, we need police to treat crimes against children as highly vulnerable to the cross-fingerpointing problem. This means always starting the investigation by immediately separating the parents and asking tough, even offensive, questions. Most innocent parents won't mind, guilty ones will, and skilled police officers will be able to tell the difference and use it to their investigative advantage.

We also need new ethical restraints that forbid defense attorneys from falsely pointing the finger of blame at an innocent person. It's one thing to claim that some unknown person is the real killer, but implicating a real individual who the defense knows to be innocent is wrong. These so-called Plan-B strategies not only pose a real risk that an innocent person may be wrongly convicted, but also, they increase the chance that criminals will drag the truly innocent into a criminal act just for cover in case they get caught. With increasing reports of criminals' planting other people's DNA at crime scenes intentionally to make a mess of the evidence, cross-fingerpointing tactics are likely to become even more problematic in the future. In fact, advancements in science are making it easier, not harder, for criminals and their lawyers to create reasonable doubt with unreasonable tactics.

Finally, we need to loosen ethical restrictions on prosecutors so they can proceed with a case even if they aren't sure *beyond a reasonable doubt* that they can win. This is critically important in a circumstance where the accused or his lawyer strategically creates doubts—endeavoring to deflate the weight of the state's case—by injecting false information into the public arena or the investigative process, or by interfering with the crime scene or the ability of a witness to testify truthfully at trial. Accused criminals deserve truly fair trials, but there is no constitutional value in allowing criminals to maliciously tamper with a legitimate investigation effort, or falsely prop up an innocent person as a potential suspect to bear some of the suspicion as a way of preventing a prosecution.

Cross-fingerpointing needs to stop; but this will not happen until the lawyers who recommend it to their clients as the path to freedom are treated as accomplices to crime.

Eleven

Bullying the Advocates

PEOPLE WHO SPEAK UP FOR VICTIMS IN LOW-PROFILE cases get bullied all the time—usually by the bad guy or his buddies. High-profile trials are no different. The bullies just tend to use the media to help with the harassment; and they balloon up the buddy pool, often to an astonishing extent, with the (mostly) unwitting help of defense-oriented pundits and legal analysts.

I got a ton of hate mail from people who didn't like the fact that I was on television speaking up for the victims in the Scott Peterson, Kobe Bryant, and Michael Jackson cases. I don't even read the stuff and I understand it comes with the territory: A few nuts get overly invested in these "true-crime stories" and want people like me to stop supporting the victim's point of view. Why? Well, obviously because they want their hero to prevail in court and go free. But it's also because a lot of folks simply don't want to believe anything bad about some of the people who get charged with serious crimes in this country.

At this point, it may be worth distinguishing between the two major categories of bullies: professionals and amateurs. In the former category, you have defense attorneys and special-interest groups. Special-interest groups, which wield astounding amounts of power in our society, try as hard as they can to influence public debates to their advantage. That's their job. And when you stop and think about it, most special interests are directly affected by the actions of our court system.

The amateurs come into play when a bunch of like-minded people form an ad hoc group to achieve a certain goal. (I don't mean amateur in a pejorative sense; I simply mean people other than the professionals who advocate for a cause.) Sometimes the effort is focused on a person whom they believe to have been wrongly charged with a crime. Some are paid, others just have too much time on their hands. When I step in to advocate for a victim in a high-profile case, the e-mails, letters, and phone calls from both types of bullies start to fly.

Both the special-interest and ad hoc groups send tons of e-mails to people like me most often to complain but sometimes to express their appreciation. The angry e-mails tend to come in by the bushel; the thank-you notes come in by ones and twos.

Frankly, neither the criticisms nor the compliments influence my work at all. Victim advocates like me expect criticism from certain people, and we're not doing this work because we're look-ing for applause. We stand up for all victims; and we don't care if they're rich or poor, black or white, male or female. Let me add a caveat here. There are some advocates who only support certain categories of victims, and only in certain kinds of cases. More on this in Chapter 13.

Back to bullies: I wish I could say that bullying never works to silence anyone because it shouldn't—but, unfortunately, that's not always the case. When the intimidation gets intense and the people who support the accused are especially powerful bullies, victim advocates sometimes go silent.

When I'm tempted to go silent, I remind myself that when the bad guy is powerful, the person for whom I'm advocating doesn't usually have many allies, and more often than not, he or she has a multitude of newfound enemies. Whatever pressure I'm feeling as an attorney for a victim-client or as a pundit on televi-sion, the victim is feeling that pressure a hundred times over. Even when I'm getting threatened with lawsuits, I keep in mind that the victim may be getting death threats.

As a lawyer who fights for victims, I realize it's my job to stay on task—no matter how unpopular my client or my argument in the court of popular opinion. Wouldn't you do the same for your client? What if the victim was your daughter, and you knew that she was telling the truth, but everyone supported the perpetrator because he was famous or a star athlete at school? Would you stop supporting your child? Of course not. When it's someone else's child, aren't we, as Americans, supposed to hold off judg-ment and support the idea that everyone—no matter what their station in life—deserves their day in court, including even unlikable victims? The sad thing is, defense attorneys who claim to care about constitutional freedoms are often the first ones in line to trounce on the Constitution by using threats and bully tactics to silence the free-speech rights of their opposition.

Let me distinguish between "fighting" and "bullying." I love a good fight, and I respect skilled adversaries, even when (especially when) I lose the debate. When both sides play by the rules, a good fight can actually serve a purpose beyond the entertainment value of two smart lawyers sparring for sport. Whether it's clarifying the key issues in a no-profile case or educating the public on policy issues or larger legal principles at stake in a high-profile case, most lawyers understand the power of a healthy disagreement and we certainly don't take it—or dish it—personally. That's why after I have a heated battle with a defense attorney on a TV talk show or news segment, that attorney and I may wind up socializing after the show ends. One of my fiercest defense combatants on the air, Jayne Weintraub, is a longtime personal friend. I've been to her home; she sent me a lovely baby gift when my last child was born; and we help each other with real-world cases. Yes, Jayne represents people who make my skin crawl—and I'm proud of her for that. In fact, I wouldn't have it any other way.

But some defense lawyers are just bullies. They suffer from what I call the I-can't-win-the-argument-so-I'll-just-whack-my-opponents-around-with-a-bat syndrome. Typically, they start with the victims themselves, using the intimidation tactics described earlier. Then they move on to the next circle out, which includes victim advocates like me. I've developed many a migraine headache because of jerks who acted less like licensed, legal professionals and more like the uncivilized clients they were representing. A few years ago, a lawyer on the other side of one of my high-profile cases filed an ethical complaint against me in an effort to stop me from talking to the media about a terrible injustice that had been perpetrated by his client. To nobody's great surprise, the complaint was dismissed as frivolous. I responded by talking in public about the case as loudly, as long, and as often as I could. Eventually, I won a huge victory for my client. Meanwhile, it also was a victory for the justice system that a bottom-feeding jerk of a lawyer not only failed to muzzle me but caused even more of the truth to be told, because his attempt to squelch the truth generated even greater public interest in the real story. For those of you who care about tactics that undermine truth telling, the message is an important one: The bullies don't always win.

In a more recent case of bullying, John Ramsey's lawyer, Lin Wood—during an appearance on *Larry King Live*—threatened to sue me for the opinions I had expressed about the Ramsey case moments earlier on Paula Zahn's show on CNN. What the public didn't know was that right before Wood wasted all his airtime on Larry King talking about me, he called me personally to threaten me over the phone.

I knew ahead of time that Wood was a thug because his reputation had preceded him. The phone call only confirmed that reputation. When I answered the phone, he sounded like he was making a well-rehearsed speech, rather than expressing earnest concern about his client's rights. "Wendy Murphy," he began, in a bombastic twang, "this is Lin Wood. I just heard you accuse my client of abusing and killing his daughter, and if

I ever hear you say that again, you won't be ex-prosecutor Wendy Murphy, you'll be defendant Wendy Murphy in my lawsuit. Check my record!"

In response to which I said, "Check your record? Kiss my a--!" Then I told him he had a lot of nerve threatening me. And after I hung up the phone, I found myself grinning a bit. Something I said must have hit a nerve in order to get this guy so riled up.

What got Wood going, you wonder? He had heard me state my opinion that John Ramsey was involved in the death of his daughter, by accident, in a sexual incident that could have been connected to child pornography. I explained that the pornography angle wasn't my theory, but, in fact, police had executed multiple search warrants related to child pornography in the early days of the investigation. Police searched for child pornography in their summer home in Charlevoix, Michigan, a house located by a body of water that leads to the Canadian border. Police also searched on the Ramseys' personal and professional computers. Police later said they found no pornography in the home. The list of items taken off the computers was filed with the court but does not indicate whether anything incriminating was uncovered. Just because no porn was found in the home doesn't mean there isn't a porn connection to the case.

As I explained on Paula Zahn's show, in the ugly world of child pornography, pictures of a young, fake-blonde (the Ramseys bleached the child's hair to make it light blond), gorgeous child—with S and M features such as a ligature around the neck—are among the pictures most prized by perverts. Famed forensic medical examiner Dr. Cyril Wecht studied the autopsy report and some of the evidence and opined in his book on the Ramsey case that JonBenet died accidentally from strangulation, and that the use of the ligature may have been related to a sadistic sexual event. As an expert in the field of sexual violence, I know that child pornography is a multibillion-dollar industry, and that—according to United States Attorney General Alberto Gonzalez—the most common producers of child porn are the victim's parents.

No, all of this doesn't mean the Ramseys are guilty, but it's certainly relevant and fair to talk about these things and to try to connect the dots and debate potential theories about what happened. The Ramseys themselves did exactly this when innocent men were being accused of the crime. It's interesting, isn't it, that it's okay for them to discuss theories about innocent strangers being involved, but it's not okay for other people to discuss theories about the Ramseys' possible involvement, even when the evidence disproves the so-called intruder theory.

As I also explained on CNN right before Wood blew a gasket, people should not be misled into believing that JonBenet was killed by a stranger, in light of the autopsy findings that revealed evidence of "acute" and "chronic" vaginal trauma. This means the child had new and old genital injuries. The child's vaginal insides were described as showing epithelial erosion and chronic irritation. Her hymen was eroded, and damaged to the point where only a small piece remained intact. Let me repeat, neither of the Ramseys has ever been charged with anything. But if JonBenet was killed by the same person responsible for causing her chronic vaginal injuries, then the murderer had to have been someone who had ongoing intimate access to the little girl.

A lot of people have long wondered about the connection between this evidence and the fact that JonBenet had reportedly been to the pediatrician nearly thirty times between the ages of three and six. Several of those visits were for genital irritation and vaginal discomfort. Coincidence? Maybe. But child-abuse experts will tell you that mothers sometimes bring an abused child to an outside professional as a disguised cry for help. Sometimes a mother feels afraid or personally incapable of protecting her child from harm, so she brings the child to a doctor or teacher or social worker in the hope that person will ask the child appropriate questions to determine whether something harmful is going on at home.

JonBenet's pediatrician at the time said he saw no signs of abuse though he never conducted an internal examination, which means he would not have seen the epithelial erosion or the eroded hymen. Of course, the visits to the pediatrician may have had nothing to do with anything and theories abound concerning who murdered the child and why.

The strange thing is, Lin Wood doesn't seem to have any problem with the countless crazy theories and false statements that have been dumped into the public arena, theories that undermine a search for the truth. If he and the Ramseys really cared about finding the real killer, they sure wouldn't want nonsense about fake suspects making a bigger mess out of an already complicated case, and Lin Wood would take steps to silence the folks spewing this garbage. But he doesn't go after the people who are bogging down the case, diverting resources and wasting time on wacky information.

Nope. Wood threatens to file lawsuits to silence only certain people from articulating certain theories about the case. All the crazies can keep talking and talking and talking. Who do you think benefits from this selective bullying technique? The public? The people trying to speak for JonBenet? The cops trying to do justice for an innocent child? Not a chance.

Nobody should be threatened with harm, financial or otherwise, for articulating an opinion about a matter of great public interest, such as the brutal murder of a defenseless child in her own home. But that's exactly what people like Lin Wood do when they don't like what someone is saying. And it's not unlike what fascist extremists do when they try to maintain political power and control people by telling them about all the horrible things that will happen if they don't speak and think a certain way and live according to the rules of the dictator.

Lin Wood claims to be driven by principle, in trying to protect his client from the harsh opinions of others, but his principles must have been on vacation when he was representing the victim in the Kobe Bryant case. Wood was well aware of the false claim that his client had "sex with three men in three days" around the time of the incident; but Wood never went on CNN to threaten to sue anyone for causing additional harm to his already traumatized client.

If the victim had been my client, I would at least have filed ethical complaints against the defense lawyers—lawsuits, if necessary—and I'd have gone on every talk show to tell the truth and to denounce such slime tactics. Lin Wood and his "principled" ilk did none of this.

I don't know why Lin Wood was reluctant to criticize Bryant's lawyers about the "sex-with-three-men-in-three-days" comment—and I don't much care. The central point is that waffling on such important principles is even more evidence that there are no principles at work here.

It is an abomination that lawyers can so profoundly disrespect the right to free speech—a core value from which all freedoms flow—by using the law and their authority as officers of the court to pound people into silence. Even speculative and offensive opinions have value in a legitimate search for the truth. The solution to offensive speech is more speech, which means if Wood doesn't like what I'm saying, he should debate me, not threaten me.

The public is entitled to the truth about the Ramsey case, but so many questions remain unanswered—questions that, if we could discuss them openly and have full access to all the files, might give us a better understanding of what happened to Jon-Benet. Like, was the bowl of pineapple police found on the kitchen table ever tested for the presence of drugs? If so, what were the results? We know the child had undigested pineapple in her belly—which means she ate it within a couple of hours of death—yet both parents adamantly denied giving JonBenet pineapple. Why? What's so bad about the pineapple? And why did police spend so much time questioning the Ramseys about the bowl of pineapple? Why did John Ramsey feel the need to clarify during his police interview that his lawyer wanted him to explain his theory about the pineapple—which was that maybe JonBenet knew her killer and that maybe they had a snack together before the murder.

Um—okay.

And why were the parents asked about prescription drugs, specifically things like Klonopin, Xanax, Paxil, and Ativan? Why did the Ramseys' lawyers allow them to answer such probing personal questions about prescription drug use in an interview that would someday become part of the public record unless there was a good reason? If I represented someone and police wanted to ask questions about my client's use of Viagra, for example, I would object and instruct my client not to answer if I thought the question had nothing to do with the case. The Ramseys' lawyers didn't object to questions about sedatives. Why not? Maybe the questions had something to do with whether the Ramseys were sedated on the night in question—which might explain why they didn't hear any noises. But if that was the purpose of the drug questions, wouldn't police have simply said, "Did you take any prescription drugs or other sleep aids before bedtime?" and if the Ramseys said, "No," just leave it at that?

If the only questions and opinions about the Ramsey case that are allowed on the airwaves are those that make the likes of Lin Wood happy, then we're all in trouble.

This problem is not unique to the Ramsey case. Court dockets and cable news shows alike are full of examples where accused criminals get to lie with impunity about their innocence, while people who believe otherwise are forbidden to say so out loud. This is Lin Wood's America, and it is the America of all lawyers who stop at nothing to bludgeon a search for the truth.

In this particular minidrama of the Ramsey case, the good news is that people noticed how Wood overreacted to my comments, and this not only made people even more suspicious, it created its own little news story. Far from a successful silencing ploy, Wood's bluster and threats afforded me the chance to appear on more programs, where I was able to talk more about the issue and the nature of bully tactics.

Deriving accidental benefits from intentional wrongdoing is not good enough. Lawyers like Lin Wood should be reined in, and the public should rise up in protest whenever they see this sort of thing happening.

And finally, we need the media to stop indulging bullies as if somehow the public good is served when they let defense attorneys smack people around, while everyone else has to play nice in the sandbox. Enough's enough.

Truth matters.

TWELVE

Selling Unfair Punishment as Restorative Justice

ONE OF THE STRANGEST AND MOST RADICAL CRIMINAL-
loving propositions to gain momentum within the criminal justice system in decades is a theory called restorative justice, and it
is creeping its evil way into courtrooms across America.

It's evil in part because it sounds so humane and crisp, fair,
and effective. After all: What could possibly be wrong with *re-
storing* a person in the name of justice? The unpleasant truth,
though, is that this is a truly warped philosophy that allows the
most dangerous criminals to be set free early—or never be
locked up at all. By persuading folks to believe that punishment
is ineffective the public is misled to believe that giving a heinous

criminal a slap on the wrist is okay, because he and the victim are about to be restored, at which point justice will have been done.

If it weren't so cruel to victims and dangerous to society, you'd have to laugh out loud.

In the introduction, I told you about the best-known example of this strange idea. Remember Edward Cashman, the Vermont judge who sentenced Mark Hulett, a man who raped a little girl countless times over the course of four years, to only sixty days in prison? Turns out Cashman taught and promoted the theory of restorative justice in his spare time, something we the public learned only after the judge found himself in the middle of a firestorm of public criticism. And it only got worse for Cashman when he tried to justify his ridiculously lenient sentence by invoking a core tenet of restorative-justice philosophy, saying that he didn't give Hulett more time behind bars because harsh punishment and a lengthy prison sentence would accomplish nothing.

Whoa! Hold on, judge! Since when did public safety become an inadequate justification for incarceration? With judges like Cashman on the bench, is it any wonder that while the crime rate overall is fairly low in Vermont, sex crimes were up by over 60 percent in 2004, compared to the number of offenses in 2003? This is what Vermonters get in exchange for judges who promote restorative justice.

I'm sure they're grateful.

There is no uniformly accepted definition of restorative justice. The fundamental premise of this nutty idea is that punishment should be de-emphasized and prosecution avoided in favor of a negotiated nonpunitive plea deal. To facilitate this, the judge allows the criminal to barter against the psychological and financial needs of victims by fake-begging forgiveness and paying the victim some money to make the case go away.

Let me sharpen that up a little bit. Restorative justice is an approach that allows perpetrators to trade the value of an apology and a few bucks in return for the victim's acceptance of a wrist slap, which in many cases translates into the outright dismissal of serious felony charges.

This is silliness. A perpetrator should be punished, *and* he should apologize, *and* he should pay the victim money after she files a civil suit when the criminal case is over. These things are not mutually exclusive. In fact, they are intimately and productively related.

And let's get real: Logically, if a criminal apologizes mainly because he thinks it's going to get him a discount on his sentence, it isn't much of an apology anyway. So there's very little restoration going on.

The sad fact is that a lot of victims are more than happy to take any offer to avoid a stressful criminal trial, and defense attorneys have a deep vested interest in keeping strong prosecution witnesses off the witness stand. But victims are entitled to know the truth; and the truth is that restorative justice is far more beneficial to the bad guy than to the victim; and it does absolutely nothing for society at large.

Do you think Cashman is the rare example? He isn't. Judges like Cashman are promoting restorative justice in courtrooms all across the country, despite the fact that it violates a core principle of our legal system: Punishment is an appropriate and essential response to crime.

Serious violence should never be minimized, especially when we're talking about crimes like child rape, which is very difficult to uncover because kids are so easy to manipulate into silence. For the most part, children can't protect themselves from adults, and the people who violate children are extraordinarily skilled at terrorizing their victims. (They get a lot of practice, unfortunately.) When judges have a chance to actually punish one of these monsters, they have to take that opportunity to send the strongest possible message of intolerance. That judge has to say, "This behavior will not be tolerated. You are going to prison because sexual abuse of a child causes the victim harm for a lifetime. There are no second bites at the apple, and we will not allow you access to even one more child. Period."

Restorative justice sends the opposite message: Your behavior wasn't that bad. You are not going to prison because, although the child will suffer emotional harm for the rest of her life, she doesn't have any broken bones. We will give you another chance because we forgive you. You told the victim you were sorry, and you gave her some money, so we believe everyone has been restored. Let's adjourn the court proceedings, and gather around the tree in front of the courthouse for a rousing rendition of "Kumbayah."

When a child predator hears this type of message, he walks away laughing at the foolishness of anyone who thinks he'll never touch another child again. All the guy is thinking about is how glad he is that he didn't have to go to prison, where the population of potential new child victims is zero. Child–sex predators are the most manipulative, selfish, and cunning of all criminals; yet judges like Edward Cashman feed their pathology by touting the power of an apology and a hug. That's like handing a homeless alcoholic five bucks, but only after he promises to spend it on milk and cookies. Give me a break.

I'm not saying punishment is the only thing that matters or that the system doesn't need more and better treatment for all prisoners. And it would be a great idea if we could get more rapists and killers to accept responsibility for their crimes—an aspect of restorative justice that I support. It's just that we can't let the criminal justice system become a marketplace, in which negotiating the punishment for a despicable crime is treated like a real estate deal or a corporate transaction. I'll say it again: Justice should be better than capitalism.

To appreciate how ridiculous the concept of restorative justice really is, it's important to remember that "criminal justice" is not just a phrase attached to the process by which we grind out convictions and stash the guilty people behind bars. It essentially means truth and fairness in the redress of serious public wrongdoing, and it is a core concept around which our society is organized. Justice is a philosophical backbone from which we draw inspiration about the value of humanity and derive direction about how to treat one another with civility and respect. This means that how we do justice is both a message sender and a mirror on our collective beliefs. What do we think is valuable enough to be worthy of meaningful protection, and are we conveying a clear message about our choices in the way crimes are being processed and punished? When the justice system does something the public sees as unfair, civility suffers. Respect for law suffers. In fact, the only one who doesn't suffer is the criminal. How is this good for society, or fair, or wise?

Restorative-justice types are right about at least one thing: The system is broken. But it isn't broken in a way that requires us to go easy on criminals. On the contrary, the system is broken because criminals and their lawyers have had the courts by the throat for far too long. We don't need more coddling of the bad guys. We need reforms that give back some measure of legitimacy to a system that, at least since the O. J. Simpson trial, has had people in other nations laughing at us even as we boast about our superiority.

Restorative justice literally decriminalizes violence by reducing the personal costs criminals are expected to endure as payment for their crimes. It doesn't take a lot of deep reflection to see how making crimes cheaper to commit makes them easier to commit.

Nor is it hard to see how minimizing punishment will reduce the value of human life by rendering the power of law impotent to promote the essential value of mutual respect in society.

Certain kinds of crimes, especially sex crimes against children, are out of control in this country. We desperately need the exact opposite of what restorative justice offers. I might feel differently if scientifically valid data proved that restorative justice actually reduced crime in some way, but there is simply no good evidence that it does anything at all to prevent recidivist violence.

Take juvenile offenders, for example. We tried a restorative approach for a long time, and it didn't work. Reasonable people argued that when it comes to kids who commit crimes, we should look hard at creative, nonpunitive alternatives to incarceration.

After all, kids are less morally culpable than adults, and they are certainly more fixable. Their brains aren't even done growing, which suggests that maybe we can still make a difference if we get involved in the lives of troubled kids, and get them on track to achieve an education with hard work and hope for future success. Unfortunately, studies show that a restorative philosophy just doesn't work, even when it comes to juveniles. I'm not saying no child can be saved, but as a policy matter, the numbers just aren't there to justify a wholly soft-on-crime approach for criminals—no matter what their age.

During the 1970s and '80s, the criminal justice system got deeply invested in a purely rehabilitative approach to juvenile crime. Even kids who committed murder rarely suffered any real punishment or incarceration. They went into treatment and social service programs, and we spent a fortune trying to repair the mental software of kids who were getting into trouble with the law.

In the aftermath of this period, kids began committing more serious crimes, and at younger ages than ever before. One reasonable interpretation of the data is that kids got the message that they could commit virtually any crime with impunity. Rob a store—get a hug. Kill a person—go to therapy. No wonder things got worse.

Some claim that the rehabilitation model wasn't a complete failure because juvenile crime rates went down overall— although it's likely that demographic shifts explain the data. But for our purposes, that debate is beside the point. The main point is that juveniles today are more violent at younger ages than ever before, and this directly follows a period in which the juvenile justice system was primarily restorative, rather than punishment oriented.

With this experience just behind us and with states having responded across the board with new tougher laws to deal with juvenile offenders, it is shocking to see otherwise smart people promoting restorative ideas for adult criminals. It didn't work for kids. Why in the world would anyone think it would work for adults? The public's angry reaction to Judge Cashman's decision is strong evidence that society is literally on the verge of becoming violent about the idea.

Led by Bill O'Reilly on the Fox News Channel, protests of Cashman's decision emerged across the country overnight. People of all political stripes and persuasions were incredulous. Cashman tried to cover for his inane decision by suggesting he only gave Hulett sixty days behind bars because he wanted the defendant to get treatment, and treatment was only available to certain high-level offenders in prison. Low-level offenders had to wait to get help until they were released from prison, and Hulett was deemed a low-level offender.

Let's not hang up here on the absurdity of defining a man who raped a child countless times over four years as a low-level offender—although that certainly deserves some scrutiny. A fair number of people took comfort from the fact that Cashman had an explanation for the sixty-day sentence. But that comfort didn't last long as it was soon revealed that Cashman's explanation was untrue. Cashman had agreed with the defense attorney to a sentence of no more than ninety days long before it was determined whether Hulett would be deemed a low-risk or a high-risk offender. In other words, Cashman agreed to a trivial jail term long before he knew whether Hulett would be eligible for treatment in prison. It's bad enough when a judge cuts some serious slack for a confessed child rapist, but then to lie about it? I could almost respect the guy if he stuck to his guns and said, "Look—I think prison is bad for people, and I'm willing to take the heat for my ideological bias," or something like that. But he didn't have the guts to stand up for his convictions, as it were. Instead, he spun like a madman and made up a story about wanting to help sex offenders get treatment. The worst part is: A lot of folks in Vermont bought it.

Several newspapers made Cashman out to be some kind of folk hero—touting the judge for using the Hulett case to pressure the prison system to make treatment available to all levels of sex criminals. The Vermont Press Association even gave the guy a First Amendment award in the fall of 2006 for his commitment to "openness in government." I kid you not. When I first heard he got this award, I thought it was a joke. Shouldn't an award in the name of the First Amendment be saved for government officials who at least tell the truth about how they conduct the business of the people?

This type of behavior gives fuel to the fire that the media has an intentional liberal antiprosecution bias aimed at rewarding judges who promote criminals' rights no matter what the cost. I can understand this mind-set to some extent. After all, the fourth estate is supposed to provide a check against unfair government power. This is a good thing. But what about holding the government accountable when it systematically fails to redress targeted violence against defenseless children? After 9/11, the liberal media has supported prosecutions and harsh punishments for hate-motivated violence against Muslims and Arabs. This helps to hold judges and prosecutors accountable for responsible enforcement of criminal laws, which, in turn, helps deter hate crimes. What I want to know is, how come the media doesn't see itself as having a similar responsibility to watch over the government's inertia when it comes to other forms of targeted violence—especially violence against voiceless kids?

In my opinion, the award wasn't so much an award for Cashman as a punishment of Bill O'Reilly. The Vermont media knew that O'Reilly had exposed a terrible injustice and brought well-deserved shame to bear on the entire state of Vermont. Lots of good people there were mortified by Cashman's conduct, but many in power were cheering the idea that a judge refused to incarcerate a dangerous criminal, and they were furious with O'Reilly. So the press gave Cashman a prize. Sick, I know. And the funny thing is: It not only won't stop O'Reilly, it will probably ramp up the amount of attention he pays to Vermont's justice system now that it looks like the local media is committed to celebrating judges like Edward Cashman.

Again, I wouldn't have minded nearly as much if Cashman legitimately wanted to pressure the system to provide more treatment for all prisoners. I admire people who care about helping criminals reform their lives. My brother's childhood friend got involved with drugs as a young man and his addiction led to repeated incarcerations—mostly for driving under the influence of drugs. His wife breathed a sigh of relief when he got locked up because she knew he would at least be safe for a while. After he wrapped up a sentence, he'd stay sober for a time; but the addiction was too strong, and he'd get in trouble again. The last time he got out, he told his wife he'd stay clean forever. And, in fact, he really wanted to. He had two little kids, and he knew his addiction was hurting them more than anyone else. He didn't last long before dying from an overdose. Everyone who knew him said he might have had a chance if there had been treatment available in prison and good follow-up care on the outside. We'll never know.

So sympathy for criminals isn't ridiculous, but Cashman stepped way over the line from sympathy to lunacy, and the protests against him became so intense that Cashman was forced to increase Hulett's sentence from sixty days to three years. Even that was nowhere near enough. It also was a case of too little too late. The harsh criticism of Cashman continued, and he eventually resigned from the bench in the fall of 2006.

I had already been working with Bill O'Reilly for a while when all of this transpired. He had hired me to help with his Jessica's Law campaign, which was an effort to get all fifty states to adopt tough mandatory minimum punishments for child–sex predators. Jessica's Law—or more formally, the Jessica Lunsford Act—was passed unanimously by both houses of the Florida legislature in the spring of 2005. It imposes mandatory sentences on child molesters and requires sex offenders released from prison to wear GPS tracking devices for the rest of their lives. Together, we covered the Cashman case extensively, and when the pressure finally forced Cashman to increase the guy's sentence, I told Bill something he didn't even realize: As far as I knew, no judge had ever before increased a criminal's punishment in response to public outcry. This was truly a watershed moment in the American criminal justice system and it wasn't a prosecutor or an appellate court or a legislature that made it happen—O'Reilly made it happen.

Of course, I had seen cases where the opposite happened—when public outcry caused a convicted criminal to have a sentence reduced. Take, for example, the prosecution of Louise Woodward, the so-called Nanny Trial that I mentioned in Chapter 8. Massachusetts Judge Hiller Zobel allowed Woodward to walk free the very same day she was convicted of murdering baby Matty Eappen. Large crowds of Woodward supporters had gathered outside the courthouse over the course of the multiweek trial, some of whom had reportedly been paid to be there. Judge Zobel was certainly well aware of these crowds when he reduced Woodward's conviction from murder to manslaughter and then sentenced the baby-killer to time served and sent her home instead of to prison where she belonged.

It's not all that unusual, actually. Protests are often used to pressure governors to commute death sentences. A restive mob certainly put pressure on Judge Ito in a way that allowed the defense to get away with murder—so to speak—during the O. J. Simpson trial.

So turning up the heat on judges to go easy on criminals is nothing new; but before O'Reilly took on Cashman, no one had ever successfully pressured a judge to go *tougher* on a criminal. Aside from being a huge victory for O'Reilly, this was an important message from the public aimed directly at our entire legal system. The restorative justice stuff had exploded in Cashman's face, and people were taking to the streets. I got tons of e-mails from people about the Cashman situation asking what they could do to help. Some were so angry that they talked about vigilantism as the only answer. I always discourage people from taking the law into their own hands. At the same time, I could sense the real fear and frustration in what people were saying about Judge Cashman.

The public is now on full alert that there are judges like Cashman all across the country, quietly doling out lenient sentences to the most dangerous criminals. Some, like Pennsylvania judge Rayford A. Means, make no mention of restorative justice, but their decisions still reflect a dangerous ideology that favors leniency over fairness and public safety. Means was chastised by his own appellate court in 2006 for giving a convicted sex offender named Tracy McIntosh a sentence of house arrest. After hearing unequivocal evidence that McIntosh was a vile rapist, Judge Means described the guy's conduct as something akin to getting drunk in public, calling the rape "bad judgment," "inappropriate," and "dishonorable behavior." Someone should have told Judge Means that—according to the United States Supreme Court—rape is the ultimate violation of self, short of murder.

Thanks to the integrity of the Pennsylvania appellate courts, the sentence of house arrest was overturned on appeal and the judge got a good tongue lashing for trying to excuse his weak sentence in terms suggestive of a restorative justice agenda. Means actually said to the convicted rapist: "I do not believe you have to be warehoused. I think you just have to be directed in the right direction." The appellate court rightly said the punishment did not "fit the crime" and that Judge Means gave "far too much weight" to "McIntosh's rehabilitative needs" compared to the needs of society and the harm to the victim.

There are many more judges like Cashman and Means out there—too many to include in this chapter—but it's important to pay attention when judges refuse to punish offenders with prison sentences proportionate to the crime. When you come across such a judge, drop me an e-mail and tell me about it. No, we can't stop judges from believing in ideas that undercut the purposes of our justice system, but we can all play a role in making sure they don't act on their personal beliefs by letting them know that we're angry, that we're watching them carefully, and that we won't stay silent.

If the people in charge care about what's good for society, someone will pull the reins in on these judges and put a stop to restorative justice before the public takes to the streets, and before the system crumbles under the weight of the public's disrespect and outrage.

Yes, I'm well aware that proponents of restorative justice insist the goal is to encourage the offender to be accountable to the victim and to society. They cite the old Native American justice system—a system that relied on shame and stigma rather than incarceration to deter future wrongdoing because there were no prisons. But if today's restorative justice proponents are right that the Native Americans were on target touting the value of stigma, then why do today's proponents of restorative justice openly oppose sex-offender registries when registries make shaming the bad guys easy and effective?

And if today's proponents really thought Native Americans had it right, they'd support long-term mandatory punishment for child rapists, because Native Americans banished those guys forever from the tribe. One strike and you're out. No feather-passing to the predators. They didn't have prisons, but banishment served the same purpose.

Let's take that lesson from the Native Americans and get Jessica's Law passed in every state—long-term mandatory punishments for child rapists the very first time they get caught. They have to face punishments that offer no fudge room so that a judge can get around the mandatory sentence by letting a perpetrator plead to some vague lesser-included crime called molestation that carries no prison time. We need one law that covers rape of a child. You violate it, you're gone, period.

To stiffen judicial backbones, we also need laws that force all judges to issue annual report cards, similar to what is already happening in Virginia and Pennsylvania. When compliance rates are publicly reported every year, the public can assess whether certain judges are more likely than others to give unjust discounts to dangerous predators. Judges who care about the integrity of the law rather than the ability to promote their own personal ideology will welcome this form of public oversight.

And finally, we need better judicial accountability by the public. This includes, for example, having individuals form citizens' groups so they can speak out quickly when judges shirk their responsibilities as public servants. Mothers Against Drunk Driving is a good example of how a citizens' group can make a difference. Through court-watch programs, publicity campaigns, and political activism, MADD has been extremely effective at holding judges accountable in drunk-driving cases.

Now we need parents to do the same thing for sex crimes.

I even have an acronym to propose for the name of the group: Mothers and Fathers Incensed over Sex Offenders, or MAFIOSO.

MAFIOSO has a nice, ominous ring to it, doesn't it? Makes it seem as though its members mean business. I know I do. Do you?

THIRTEEN

Co-opting the Public with the Victims' Rights Charade

MOST OF YOU HAVE HEARD SOMETHING ABOUT VIC-
tims' rights, even if you've never been involved in a criminal
case. But did you know that despite reams of victims' rights laws
on the law books in every state in this country, the simple fact is
these laws are almost never enforced?

And shockingly enough, most victims are never even told
they have rights, much less what they should do if their rights
are threatened or violated. In fact, I have yet to meet a person
who, before talking to me, was even aware that he or she had
rights as a crime victim.

It's actually worse than that. Victims' rights laws are mostly toothless tigers, which look good on paper but do little for the victim.

When you read the laws, they sound good enough. They say friendly and puffy things like, "The victim has the right to be treated with dignity and respect." Well, okay, but I have yet to see a judge order anyone to respect the victim or restore the victim's dignity when a perpetrator harasses a victim's friends and family, or when a defense attorney gratuitously insults a victim during trial or violates her privacy by asking irrelevant questions about her personal life.

One of the most common tenets of victims' rights—and among the most ignored and violated—is the one that promises victims a speedy trial. Some states call it a right to a prompt disposition. The name really doesn't matter, because the point is promptness for the victim is typically ignored in favor of defense-manufactured delays that are designed to drag the case out until all the witnesses drop dead.

Victims' rights laws are often ignored because in most states these laws contain a sneaky clause, stuck somewhere toward the end, that typically says—in so many words—none of the aforementioned rights shall be enforceable.

No, there's no typo there; that's what the laws say.

So what I want to know is, who in their right mind passes a law and makes it unenforceable the same day? Just imagine the outrage if such a clause had been added to a law giving women the right to vote. Sure you can vote—just don't actually show up on election day because we might not let you vote and there's nothing you can do about it.

What's wrong with all the happy talk in this type of unenforceable legislation? In my opinion, a law with no teeth is actually worse than no law at all, because it's patronizing and because it sets in stone the idea that victims don't need or are not worthy of real rights. And it truly is the ultimate in dirty tricks when legislators—often lawyers—dupe people into believing they've just enacted a terrific new victim-oriented law when in reality they were dealing victims a colossal insult.

Of course, not everything in the law books can or should be equally enforceable. Let's face it: Even though the pursuit of happiness is in the Declaration of Independence, you can't exactly march into court and file a lawsuit when you're not feeling chipper. But it is downright un-American to co-opt people into silence by making them think they have rights when, in fact, they have nothing but nice-sounding legal mumbo jumbo.

If victims' rights were enforceable, it would never have taken more than three years for Robert Blake's case to come to trial because the judge would have been compelled to respect the victim's speedy trial rights. (Yes, the law says that even homicide victims have rights—they belong to surviving family members.)

If victims' rights were enforceable, Rhode Island Judge Francis Darigan never could have agreed to a plea deal in 2006 for the owners of a nightclub whose use of dangerous insulation led to the deaths of a hundred people in a tragic fire. The judge gave the owners a deal—one got no prison time at all—before hearing from the victims' families, even though the law provides that victims have a right to make an impact statement *before* the sentence is determined.

If victims' rights were enforceable, the lawyer for convicted kidnapper Stephen Fagan never could have gotten away with disrespecting the victim during Fagan's sentencing hearing after his 1999 conviction. Fagan kidnapped his two young daughters from their mother when they were very young, then fled to Florida and changed their names. When the girls were found in Massachusetts, some twenty years later, Fagan was remarried to a wealthy woman. After his arrest, Fagan hired an expensive attorney and a PR firm. Public criticism soon followed and the girls' mother was vilified for allegedly causing Fagan to kidnap the children because she was a terrible parent. It was heart wrenching to see the near-daily torturing of a woman whose life had already been ruined by the loss of her children. The children, by this point both young women, couldn't be expected to care about their mother's feelings. They'd been living with their kidnapper for years. It was hard for the public to feel sympathy when the children who had been wrenched from their mother's arms weren't posing for joyous reunion photo ops.

A dignified defense attorney would have appreciated the strategic benefits of having the children side with the kidnapper—and just shut his mouth about the girls' mother. After all, there is no legal justification for kidnapping. It's simply not a valid defense to say, "Well, she was a crummy parent, so I decided to steal the kids." (If that were a legitimate defense, I would have kidnapped Michael Jackson's kids a long time ago.) The judge ruled as much in Fagan's case, which meant that all the talk about the mother's problems years earlier (assuming it was true, and much of it was not) was completely irrelevant. But that didn't protect the woman from being pounded into the ground while the case was being litigated.

With public sentiment being manipulated by a money machine, hatred for the mother and sympathy for the kidnapper rose to such a level that Fagan's attorney, Richard Egbert, was able to work out a deal with the prosecutor so that his client would serve no jail time. He would plead guilty but only pay a fine and be placed on probation. After the deal was in place, the lawyers went to court to have the sentence imposed.

That's when things got really ugly. With the national news media in the courtroom, Egbert's ego took over, and his sadistic personality came to the fore. Rather than accepting the deal quietly, as an officer of the court should, he made a wild-eyed speech, going on and on about how twenty years ago, the girls' mother had psychological and other irrelevant personal problems. Now, remember, this didn't matter in the case in any way whatsoever because the judge had ruled that whatever problems the parents had in their personal lives, they were irrelevant to the crime of kidnapping. Period.

So this was a relatively simple case of a man stealing two little girls from their mother. He was guilty, and he was getting a great deal. He should just take his gift and go home, right? Wrong. Egbert babbled on and on about the mother's past with television cameras in the room for all the world to hear. She sat there, silent and dignified, while he slapped her around. The fact that Egbert's client had ruined this woman's life decades earlier wasn't bad enough; Egbert wanted her to be embarrassed on the world stage. Open up that wound, grab a pile of salt, and rub it right in. Nice.

This is a perfect example of how if victims' rights laws had any value, a lawyer for the mother could have jumped up and objected. If victims had a real right to be treated with dignity, or even a minimal way of demanding respect for privacy, someone could have stopped Egbert before he started. Egbert knew full well that what he was saying was deeply personal and had been ruled irrelevant. The prosecutor knew, too, as did the judge; but without meaningful victims' rights laws, nobody did anything to stop it.

In case after case, where victims try to complain about their rights being violated, judges tell them they have no standing. "You're not a party to the case," they say. But just because a victim isn't a party to the criminal case doesn't mean the judge shouldn't be required to listen when a victim has a complaint and then do something about it. The problem is that most judges won't take the time, not only because victims' rights aren't enforceable at the trial court level but also because there's no right of appeal in most states. That means: If the judge refuses to do anything or gets it badly wrong, there's no recourse for the victim. Is it any wonder judges don't take the time?

This is why lawyers like me, as well as people associated with the federally funded National Crime Victim's Law Institute, spend so much time fighting for amendments to victims' rights laws. We're trying to get rid of unenforceability clauses so that things like the right to a speedy trial and the right to be treated with dignity and respect will have teeth.

This is also why I spend so much time teaching victims about other, enforceable rights; laws that have nothing to do with victims' rights statutes. These include things like privacy and due process rights. I teach an idea I call the victim's privacy

Miranda rights, which involves telling victims they have the right to say "none of your damn business" when anyone involved in a criminal case asks a probing, irrelevant question about their personal life. If accused criminals can be empowered by regular Miranda laws to refuse to answer all questions during an investigation, then innocent citizens should be authorized to resist unfair questions.

What victims really need, rather than unenforceable rights, is a way to ensure their privacy and safety, as soon as possible in the aftermath of criminal violence. A personal attorney can help do this and can speak publicly and insulate the victim from media pressure and intimidation tactics, which is an especially important consideration in high-profile cases.

Naysayers and defense attorneys often denigrate lawyers who work for victims by suggesting that victims' lawyers see dollar signs in a potential civil suit after the criminal trial is over. Sometimes this is true. But a lot of lawyers help victims for no financial reward. For example, scores of plaintiff attorneys from the American Trial Lawyers Association donated countless hours of legal services to the victims of 9/11 and their families. These lawyers knew victims' families would need compensation as quickly as possible so they could pay the rent, buy food, and obtain desperately needed medical and psychological care. While the lawyers could have asked for compensation, every single one of them willingly waived their fees—a service worth many millions of dollars. Few people even know about this story because the lawyers who donated their time also refused to accept recognition for their generosity.

Unfortunately, this high-minded—even noble—approach

to lawyering is harder to find when it comes to the representation of victims in more run-of-the-mill criminal cases. Lawyers like me understand this, which is why we roll our eyes when defense attorneys claim that we're in it for the money. Funny thing, though: When a lucrative civil settlement on behalf of a crime victim is possible, the greedy shark lawyers do tend to come out of the woodwork—including those who otherwise represent criminals and bad-mouth their victims.

Attorney Joe Tacopina from New York, for example, routinely insults crime victims and shills for the defense as a pundit on cable news shows. But when he was offered the chance to make a ton of money by representing the family of Imette St. Guillen—the young woman who was brutally raped and murdered allegedly by a bouncer at a New York bar in 2006—Tacopina was only too happy to change his tune, start trashing the bad guys, and sing the woes of victims. It will be interesting to see how much the case settles for, since that will give us a good perspective on the going rate for a defense attorney's soul.

Victims and their families are free to hire whomever they want. There's certainly nothing illegal or unethical about Tacopina representing a crime victim, no matter how much he insults other victims on television. But it would sure help the good guys if victims and their families did a little research before deciding whom to hire. If a lawsuit is possible and a victim hires a lawyer or a law firm that sometimes represents criminals and/or insurance companies, the fees will go to lawyers who all too often work against the interests of victims. Alternatively, if victims' families hire a lawyer or firm that refuses to represent criminals and insurance companies, the lawyer's fees are far more likely to be used to help other victims in need.

Settlement money that goes to lawyers who are ideologically dedicated to advocacy for victims would more likely be used to support the work of organizations like the Ally Foundation. This is a nonprofit entity founded by the parents of Alexandra Zapp, who was brutally murdered by a sex offender who in any rational universe would have been behind bars at the time of the crime. The Ally Foundation works tirelessly to reform sex offender laws to better protect public safety.

Another worthy organization is the It Happened to Alexa foundation, a nonprofit entity that gives money to crime victims so they can pay for travel and lodging expenses associated with their participation in criminal trials. BeyondMissing.org is another wonderful organization, founded by Marc Klaas in honor of his daughter Polly, who was murdered by a sex predator. Marc's foundation is uniquely dedicated to helping find missing kids and making sure perpetrators are captured quickly and prosecuted successfully. Protect.org is also a terrific pro-victim/ pro-prosecution group that works with legislatures around the country to repair arcane laws—such as overly tight statutes of limitation and laws that punish child pornography crimes as misdemeanors—that make it difficult to protect children from sex crimes. AngelaShelton.org helps victims help themselves with a variety of empowering information that makes accessing justice a reality for those who have no idea where to begin. Bikers Against Child Abuse (bacausa.org) is a fabulous organization of tough guys and tough women who do countless great things to promote child safety, including literally showing up on motorcycles to physically protect an endangerd child. Justice for Children is the best pro-prosecution child advocacy organization in the country. And finally, the Maryland Crime Victims' Resource Center provides excellent information and services to support and advocate for the rights of crime victims and their families.

All these organizations would fare better, financially, if civil cases arising out of criminal violence were only referred to lawyers who have a dedicated record of putting victims at the top of their list of priorities by refusing to represent criminals and insurance companies.

If you're thinking about supporting organizations that help victims, it's important to keep in mind that some people who claim to do victims' rights work, actually work against the interests of victims. They go out of their way to discourage victims from reporting crimes and testifying in criminal cases because they've been misled to believe prosecution is not an important part of violence prevention. They don't say this, of course. Most advocates say they support prosecution efforts, but just look at the silence from victim advocates in response to the Judge Cashman situation in Vermont. What was that about?

Of course, I'm not saying that these groups are not well intentioned. It's just that there's more at stake than what's happening to one victim in one case and advocates should want prosecutors to do a better job prosecuting more offenders. Not all government action is oppressive. In fact, civil rights laws, like criminal prosecutions, are a form of government power that liberates people by protecting them from harm. And let's be honest: the epidemic of sexual violence committed against women and children by private citizens is arguably more harmful to individual freedom than anything the government is doing to prosecute criminals. Isn't that a good reason to demand more government action against abusive private citizens?

There is good news to report. Dissension is growing in the ranks of victims' advocacy groups, mainly because the soft-on-crime approach hasn't worked at all and people are fed up. With thirty years of relatively ineffective reforms behind us, new voices are joining the ranks, insisting that we not waste any more time on the old ways of thinking. New leaders are rising above stale ideas of the past and are fighting for ways to give victims real power in the criminal justice system, power that will have a significant impact on violence prevention by making the criminals more fearful of prosecution. The advocates who support this philosophy deserve lots of credit for putting public safety above politics and personal interests because, let's face it, improvements in prosecution rates will reduce crime rates and put some victim advocates out of business.

In the meantime, we need more victim lawyers involved in criminal cases from the get-go. Victims should have lawyers accompany them to the police station when a crime is being reported to ensure that police conduct the best and fairest possible investigation. (And why not? Criminals' lawyers often accompany their clients to police stations to undermine police investigations.) And victim lawyers should be helping prosecutors by appearing in court when appropriate to represent the victim's personal rights and interests.

I'm confident that, together, we can make victims' rights laws work the way they're supposed to in every criminal case.

Just watch the horror stories about violations of victims' rights disappear from the headlines when crime victims everywhere show up with a lawyer like me by their side—at every police interview, every court proceeding, every sentencing hearing— ready to do battle with any defense attorney who steps over the line.

FOURTEEN

Claiming a Suspect Passed a Polygraph

DEFENSE ATTORNEYS LOVE TO MAKE NOISY ANnouncements about how their clients have passed a polygraph test. For most of us, this conjures up images of hard-nosed police hooking up the lie detector in the station house under that single, unshaded bulb hanging from the ceiling, and practically daring the subject to tell even the smallest white lie. We put a lot of stock in the claims about passing polygraphs because we think they must measure the truth. Who could possibly stay cool enough not to be uncovered as a liar in such intimidating circumstances?

Even though polygraph exams are not admissible in most

courts, police and criminals alike know that a well-done lie detector test can reveal whether a suspect is being truthful. That is why, during an investigation, cops often ask a suspect whether he is willing to submit to a lie detector. If he says "absolutely—right now!" police usually look elsewhere for the real criminal. But if he says maybe, or "okay, but in a few days," or, "I would but my lawyer advised me not to," then you know you're looking at a guy who's probably guilty as sin. And if the guy does sit for a police-administered polygraph—and he passes—you're also looking at a guy who's probably innocent.

There are no absolutes with lie detector machines, which makes sense because they don't really measure truth anyway. They measure heart rate, sweat, and physiological responses to questions—but not truth. So we shouldn't think of these machines as having slam-dunk power one way or the other.

But we should be extra suspicious when it isn't the police talking about the results but rather the suspect or his lawyer—who paid an "expert" to conduct the test under conditions not subjected to police oversight and inspection. Law enforcement officials everywhere will tell you that while polygraphs are not perfect, there are far more false negatives (guilty people passing the test) than there are false positives (innocent people failing them).

That's because police polygraphs are subjected to all kinds of rules and restrictions, while defense attorneys are under no obligation to conduct polygraphs under any specified conditions. A defense attorney can claim a suspect passed a polygraph even if the way the test was conducted makes the results downright fraudulent. Bottom line: The lack of outside oversight when suspects get private polygraph tests makes defense claims about suspects passing the tests utterly meaningless.

This is why you don't hear defense attorneys talk much about the test conditions. You hear all about the credentials of the expert who administered the test and about how many years he worked in law enforcement—the implication being that as a former cop, everything he says and does must be legitimate. But remember: These are the same defense attorneys who routinely insult law enforcement personnel and claim they can't ever be trusted to tell the truth. Police "lie all the time," according to the defense mantra—one even came up with an offensive new word, accusing cops of "testilying." I guess this is a problem for defense attorneys only when the cop is trying to solve a criminal case. When an ex-cop is trying to help a guilty guy go free by screwing with the integrity of a polygraph test, there's no talk about "testilying"—only accolades for the superpowered value of polygraph results because who could possibly question the test results of a polygraph that was administered by an ex-cop?

Um, I would—and so should you.

It doesn't matter who conducted the test if the conditions of the examination were poor. According to longtime polygrapher Jack Nasuti, you need to know details about the machine, test preparation (including the pretest interview), the condition of the person being examined, the types of questions asked, and— perhaps most important of all—whether the suspect learned how to fake the results in any way, whether through the ingestion of drugs or other substances or by learning how to trick the machine with techniques widely available on the Internet.

Remember, a polygraph machine doesn't actually measure

truth, which means that if a suspect can manipulate the test's measurement of physiological functions, or if he can dampen the feelings of guilt-associated lying, the test results can be significantly affected to produce a false result. And keep in mind that a sociopathic criminal with no conscience doesn't feel guilt and, therefore, may falsely pass a test without rigging it. This is rare, but it's possible. In one infamous example known as the Utah church bombings murder case, the suspect initially claimed he was innocent and that his polygraph results proved it. The same guy ultimately pleaded guilty to murder. I don't know if the guy was a sociopath, but I'm certain his polygraph test produced a false result.

John and Patsy Ramsey claimed that a polygraph examination proved their innocence, too, though they didn't even take one until some three years after JonBenet was murdered. Any honest defense attorney will tell you that guilty criminals never take polygraphs right away because, although most people can eventually learn how to beat the machine, it's a whole lot easier to pull off two or three years after the crime when you've had a lot of preparation time.

When the Ramseys finally did hire someone to give them a test, the first result was reportedly inconclusive. After another test, they claimed to have passed, but the full details have never been revealed; and the little that is known suggests the test conducted was more consistent with the wrong way to conduct an examination than the right way.

A proper question should usually be short, and it shouldn't contain words that have loose meanings. This generally means it shouldn't seek answers to questions about a person's state of mind.

For example, a good question would be, "Did you kill JonBenet?" Not a lot of wriggle room there. Instead, according to the sketchy details that have been released, the Ramseys were asked long, murky questions like, "Did you inflict any of the injuries that caused the death of JonBenet?" And, "Regarding JonBenet, did you inflict any of the injuries that caused her death?" And, "Regarding JonBenet, do you know for sure who killed her?"

Adding extra words and fuzzy terms like "regarding," "for sure," "inflict," and "injuries" is not appropriate for a polygraph exam because it gives the mind of the test subject time and definitional "space" within which to wander. Short, direct questions are better because the subject is forced to focus only on the topic precisely stated.

The test is also dependent on the nature of the "known truthful" standard by which responses to the test questions are compared. If the known truthful comparison is more of a murky half-truth, then all misleading or false answers to the test questions will necessarily look more like a truthful answer. For example, if the known truthful standard is, "Did you recently move to Main Street?" and you moved to Main Street six months ago, the truthfulness measurement would be affected by the murkiness of the word "recently."

We'll probably never know whether the Ramseys learned any of the tricks people use to beat the machine. For example, if you put a tack in your shoe and you poke your toe with it when asked the known truthful question—such as, "Is your name John?"—the pain will cause an increase in heart rate and perspiration. If you do the same thing when you answer no to a test question—such as, "Did you kill JonBenet?" your answer will appear truthful because it will measure up to look like a match to the known truthful question.

Full details of the Ramseys' test conditions have not been released. Nor has there been any independent analysis of the results, although the examiner acknowledged that he did not require the Ramseys to submit to a drug test to determine whether they were under the influence of any substance at the time of the test.

We also don't know what the pretest interview of the Ramseys was like—or whether there *was* one. Jack Nasuti says this is an important part of the process because it allows the examiner to get the person being tested to focus on the matter at hand. During the pretest interview, the examiner reveals his awareness of the facts of the case—including the most damning evidence—to let the individual being tested know that the guy running the machine is tuned in to the case and will notice even the slightest deception. This also gets the test subject thinking about the details and specific facts of the crime, which helps the examiner get a more honest reaction when questions about the incident are asked during the formal testing process. What all this means is that a pretest interview is important—but we don't know whether the Ramseys even had one, much less how it was conducted by their expert.

Maybe most interesting is that despite the Ramseys' apparent willingness to submit to a polygraph at the hands of their own hired guns, they never submitted to an FBI-administered test, even after promising on national television that they would do anything asked of them. Maybe this is because police have ways of administering polygraphs to prevent the suspect from distorting the results.

I have no way of knowing whether the Ramseys' polygraph results are legitimate, but a lot of questions remain unanswered, and I've learned to be suspicious of anyone who refuses to submit to a police-administered examination while claiming publicly that they've been proved innocent by their own polygraph expert.

Paid experts on polygraphs and other topics are everywhere in our legal system, and they usually provide a valuable service to the court because they bring reasonably objective and specialized knowledge to help jurors find the truth on what are often unusual, complicated or highly technical, factual disputes. But in too many cases, the goal is not elucidation but distortion. And when distortion comes in expert or scientific packaging, it's harder for jurors and the public in general to be skeptical.

Our justice system needs a way to keep the gates open wide enough so that dignified experts are allowed in but not so wide that the tricksters walk through, too. Without strict standards, not only will we continue to see scientific distortion, but taxpayers' dollars will go to waste as indigent defendants insist on more of the public's money to pay for experts on every imaginable issue. Even the not-so-indigent will take advantage. Scott Peterson's defense team scored over $225,000 in tax dollars to hire experts on God knows how many issues. Can you remember a single thing any one of them did to help the defense? Neither can I. Professional licensing boards have to step in and set standards that forbid people to serve as experts if their intention is to misstate or manipulate the truth or just make a few bucks off the public trust. It hurts the integrity of all professionals when even one expert can't resist lying for money.

There are growing indications that the public has had its fill of hired guns in the courtroom. Lawsuits against experts are more common today than ever before. Some may decry this as unfortunate, but I don't. The fact is: Experts in all fields, including polygraph examiners, will think twice before taking a big fee to manipulate the evidence or fudge the truth if they think it might cost them, not only their reputations, but maybe even their professional licenses *and* big bucks out of their own pockets.

We can all help prevent scams by remembering to be appropriately skeptical when some brash defense attorney makes big claims about some "expert" test results. The next time you hear a self-serving announcement about an accused criminal passing a polygraph, listen hard for answers to the most important questions: What were the test conditions? How much was the expert paid? Were the questions short and direct, or did the examiner use long sentences that included references to state of mind and other murky issues? Did the suspect ingest any drugs or intoxicating substances before the test? What did the pretest interview consist of? How long after the crime was committed was the polygraph test done? Did the suspect have time to learn all the tricks about how a person can falsely pass a polygraph? Did the examiner take steps to ensure the tricks weren't in use at the time of the examination? Is the expert willing to release the entire test for outside review? Were police allowed to be there for the pretest interview—and for the test itself? Were police allowed to inspect the machine and otherwise assess the testing conditions?

Chances are that when a suspect refuses a police polygraph and hires his own examiner, it wasn't much of a test at all. He didn't pass it so much as play a role in the charade, and—trust me—there were no flying colors involved.

FIFTEEN

Mounting a Not-the-Criminal-Type Defense

WHAT DO THESE TWO DEFENSE ATTORNEYS HAVE IN common?

- The lawyer who argued that his blonde babe teacher client, who raped her male student, was too pretty to go to prison
- Scott Peterson's first lawyer, who let Peterson do TV interviews in hopes that his boy-next-door look might sway public opinion

---

The answer: Both lawyers mounted the not-the-criminal-type defense. It's far from a new trick—in fact, it's been in our faces for a long time—but it seems to be gaining in popularity in the advent of round-the-clock television news.

Even the supporters of Michael Jackson, a certified creep, managed to use this trick by arguing he wasn't the type who molests children. Why? Because he loves children too much. After all, didn't he build a zoo and an amusement park at his home? Doesn't he spend all his time with kids? Doesn't that put him above suspicion?

In fact, most experts think his obsession with kids is actually a strong indicator that he is the child molester type, though a few observers actually made the reasonable point that because real pedophiles are sneaky, they're not usually dumb enough to keep child bait in their front yards.

Of course, while the public was debating whether men who build zoos in their yard are more likely to abuse kids, Jackson's lawyers were simultaneously fighting hard to prevent the jury from hearing evidence about the pop star's other victims; in other words, preventing them from figuring out from actual hard evidence about Jackson's *behavior* with children, just what type Jackson really was. You see, defense attorneys don't really mind stereotypes at all, so long as they work to the advantage of the criminal.

We should all understand by now that there's no way to look at a person and know whether he's a criminal. Most crime victims are hurt by people who don't look scary at all. Ted Bundy could have been a male model. Neil Entwistle, the British guy accused in 2006 of executing his wife and baby daughter in

Hopkinton, Massachusetts, looks like Dream Date Ken. And Alex and Derek King, the two boys from Florida who slaughtered their father, could be direct descendants of the Brady Bunch.

It's a real problem with our justice system that judges too often let criminals exploit the fact that they don't look like criminals—and, at the same time, refuse to let the prosecutor use evidence that shows what type of monster the defendant really is.

In New York State, a middle-aged attorney and married father of two was prosecuted in the mid-1990s for sodomizing his son's preadolescent friend. John Seaman claimed at his trial in that he wasn't the type who would be interested in, much less rape, a teenage boy. To rebut this, the prosecutor let the jury know that Seaman was, indeed, the type—because he had groomed the boy by showing him pornography, bathing nude with the boy, and engaging in other behaviors inconsistent with the ordinary behavior of a married attorney and father of two children. The jury convicted the guy.

So far, so good. But then an appellate court overturned the conviction in 1997 on the grounds that it was too prejudicial to let the jury hear about the porn and the nude bathing because the jury might think the guy was a sleazeball. But wasn't that the prosecution's job, especially when Seaman's defense rested in part on the contention that he was a normal, upright, law-abiding citizen?

Scott Peterson went down this road, too. When he gave an interview to Diane Sawyer, he managed to get a stream of tears flowing down his boy-next-door cheeks, while his creaky voice spewed one lie after the next. Not the type, indeed! Few people understood they were being played by a guy who wasn't man enough to submit to tough police questioning but sure didn't mind yakking up a storm with a journalist—who, like every member of the media, didn't have access to enough evidence to ask the brutal questions that would have cooked his goose, quick.

Defense attorneys think this is okay, because while the Fifth Amendment right to remain silent means the police can't talk to the suspect, it doesn't mean the suspect can't talk to—and even lie to—the press and the public. The Fifth Amendment, they claim, is a right to remain selectively silent only when it's in your best interest. Of course, this manner of testifying without taking the stand by talking to the media, thus all potential jurors, wouldn't work if the public had no interest in the case. But we are interested in cases where the perpetrator doesn't seem the murderer type. You see the conundrum? The Petersons of the world are able to taint the jury pool and whip up a mob of misguided supporters by playing against our expectations.

Sure, I understand why people are fascinated by these cases. I get fascinated, too. Let's face it: If Scott Peterson is the type of person who can slaughter his wife and nearly born son, and he looks like the guy next door (or better), then how can I protect myself and my children from dangerous people? How can I figure out who the safe people are if safe-looking people turn out like Scott Peterson? This is scary stuff to most people, and defense attorneys know it—which is why they exploit our fears whenever they can.

And yes, I can appreciate as well as anyone the profound value to civil liberties in allowing the accused to remain silent, and in making certain that jurors do not interpret that silence to the disadvantage of the accused at trial. But if this important constitutional principle is to retain its value and command its due respect, then when a suspect clams up and refuses to speak to police, he has to shut up. Period. No television, no radio, no BS about wanting to speak publicly to help find the real killer. Just shut up. The right to remain silent is a right to say nothing. It is not a right to lie.

More than ever before, with 24/7 news coverage on all high-profile trials, the public is getting bogus information from defendants and then pundits and legal analysts who discuss and spin the lies. The inevitable results? Important cases come to be decided more like beauty contests than serious legal controversies. Recall the celebratory coverage of child rapist Mary Kay Letourneau.

Letourneau was a grade-school teacher in her mid-thirties and a married mother of four young children when she decided it was appropriate to become sexually involved with her twelve-year-old student, Villi Fulaau. She was prosecuted and convicted of child rape in 1997 and then found herself pregnant at an age when Fulaau wasn't remotely old enough to make a truly free decision about engaging in sexual behavior, much less understand or handle the serious nature of fatherhood. Letourneau repeatedly defied the court's orders to stay away from Fulaau and violated her probation, which landed her back in prison where she gave birth to another of Fulaau's children. When she got out, Fulaau was old enough to make his own decisions, and he married Letourneau. A lot of people in this country talk about the situation like it's a Romeo-and-Juliet love story for the times. But what I want to know is: Why are two little kids being forced to live with parents who can't appreciate the harm of child rape? What kind of court system rewards child rapists with the gift of parenthood? What will they tell their children when they ask about how they were born. "Well dear, you see, your daddy was my student and I raped him and that's how I became pregnant with you." So sweet. I wonder who will foot the bill for the children's mental health care? And think about this—there's nothing the kids' parents can do to move to a safe neighborhood away from convicted sex offenders because mommy's a rapist.

This happened in part because we think giving birth trumps everything and that if a rapist is a woman, it can't be that bad. We think a boy can't really be harmed if his private parts feel good. Isn't this at least some of the explanation for why all the pretty blonde teachers aren't going to prison for raping fourteen-year-old boys? The truth is that rape can feel good, physically, to teenage boys, but that doesn't mean being abused by an adult is good for them. Teenage boys also like the tingly feelings they get from drinking alcohol and driving fast, but we don't say "atta boy" when they drive drunk.

Rape of a boy by a woman can be even more harmful when betrayal is involved, as when a trusted woman and mother, who is supposed to protect children, abuses her own student. The simple truth is: It's far better to let a loving man raise a child than an abusive woman. Love is more important than gender.

Letourneau also had the benefit of looking like little Lindy Loo from the Whos down in Whoville. How can a sweet-looking mother of four be dangerous? It doesn't compute, does it? So again, the joke's on us: We look at a person, think we know what type they are, and with the benefit of relentless televised romanticization of the whole mess, we cut Letourneau a lot of slack she didn't deserve. Shame on us. Instead of judging Letourneau based on her doe-eyed, petite-featured, girly face, we should have been smart enough to realize that people who deserve the privilege of raising children are the not the ones who rape them; they're the ones who put the kids' interests above their own selfish criminal fantasies.

I'm certainly not saying that news coverage of trials is always a bad thing. In fact, it's often a great thing. After all, Peterson—like a lot of dumb criminals—hurt his own case by making statements on television that were then used against him at trial. And when we're paying attention to a case, even if it's for the wrong reasons, this helps keep the heat up, not only on the suspect but also on the government, to make sure the job gets done fairly.

For example, no matter how irritated we may be about the failure of Aruban officials to solve the Natalee Holloway case since the day she went missing in May 2005, the relentless media coverage helped tremendously in pressuring the Aruban government to keep spending resources on the investigation. And we'll never tire of the Ramsey story, which means that someday her killer just might go to prison. None of this is likely to happen without television coverage.

But we need judges to stop the misuse of the press as a way for the defense to take advantage of our desire to believe that only certain types of people commit horrific acts of violence. Meanwhile, let's not let our gut-level fears and confusions about seemingly nice people trump our capacity to apply common sense and logic to the nonsense we hear on television. This really isn't all that hard to do. It requires only that we give up just a little bit of that desire to feel safe all the time.

It's okay to be suspicious of the pretty people, the rich people, and the celebrated people. It's okay to conclude that a guy who looks like Scott Peterson just might be dangerous. No, that doesn't mean he *is* dangerous. But would it be so bad if we made people *earn* our trust before deciding whether or not they're safe?

It's time to be a little bit more leery of the guy next door—even if he looks like Dream Date Ken.

Sixteen

Blaming the Victim

ALL LIFE IS PRECIOUS. WE CAN PROBABLY AGREE ON that.

Everybody—no matter how poor, or unlucky, or down-trodden—deserves a shot at happiness. By extension, nobody deserves to be a crime victim. Yes, we all have to take steps to protect ourselves and avoid engaging in risky behavior. But that doesn't mean that someone who makes a bad choice and thereby takes a risk is somehow responsible for the criminal behavior of someone else.

Unfortunately, we sometimes fail to remember this when bad things happen to people with troubled lives or to those who weren't doing their best to protect themselves when something terrible happened. All too often, we blame the victim. We react with indignation and harsh judgments when we hear that a rape victim was out having fun and—heaven forbid—drinking alcohol before the rape. And when a child is kidnapped, what's the first thing we ask? Where were the parents—as if something they did somehow caused the kidnapper to commit a crime.

This is terribly unfair and it makes no sense if we want to get tough on the bad guys. Let me be blunt. There's only 100 percent of blame to go around when crime happens. For every bit of blame we place on the victim, we necessarily reduce the criminal's responsibility. Do you really want to give a robber a break because he happened to pick on a guy who, for example, went to a bar with coworkers before the crime occurred?

Remember Imette St. Guillen, the woman I wrote about in Chapter 13, who was murdered in New York allegedly by a bouncer at a bar near her home where she'd gone for a late night drink, alone? A loud bunch of hateful people in this country said she was partly to blame for her own death because she went to a bar alone, late at night. This is simply wrong. All of our outrage should be aimed at the evil monster who tortured, raped, and murdered that poor woman.

Who in their right mind would want a judge or a jury to cut that guy any slack at all for what he did? But that's exactly what happens in the courtroom when the public harshly judges victims and accuses them of being responsible for someone else's behavior because of something they did or didn't do before the crime. Taken to its logical next step, people hit by drunk drivers are partly to blame because they could have stayed home. Similarly, store owners who get robbed bear some responsibility because they could have hired a security guard.

Nonsense! There's no way to prevent a selfish, dangerous, or desperate person from committing a crime if he wants to commit a crime. If an innocent person happens to be in the bad guy's path when the criminal mood strikes, that's only the perpetrator's fault. I don't care if a rape victim strips naked and does cartwheels down the middle of Main Street—rape is wrong. And I don't care if the elderly owner of the corner store never got around to installing a security camera. Nobody deserves to be victimized by crime.

I take it a step further. When people have problems, I see them as the underdogs in our society. I admit it. I'm a bit of a sucker for the underdog and I want the criminals who pick on them to be punished extra harshly, not given a discount. Maybe you don't agree with going this extra step. But the next time you're tempted to blame a victim, ask yourself whether the bad guy took advantage of someone with a weakness. Don't judge the weakness; just ask yourself whether the criminal jumped at the chance to pick on someone who couldn't defend himself—and then ask yourself if it makes sense to go easy on that kind of perpetrator. Then remember what I told you about why sex predators pick on kids.

I've worked on cases involving victims from all walks of life, and I can't think of a single person who deserved to be hurt. Even when pedophile priest John Geoghan was murdered in a Massachusetts prison by a man who said he did it to avenge all the harm Geoghan caused to so many children, I spoke out against that crime. I said exactly what I'm saying here: Nobody deserves to be a crime victim.

Our unfortunate propensity to be harsh toward victims is the flip side of our similarly unfortunate inclination to feel sympathy when a celebrity or influential politician stands accused of a crime. We blame the innocent when they have difficult lives, and we forgive the guilty when their lives are charmed. Go figure.

One thing I've noticed, in my twenty years of working with victims, is that when you look into someone's eyes and see pain, that pain always looks exactly the same. It really doesn't matter how important someone is: Sadness feels the same from the inside. Crime victims deserve our sympathy *and* our support. And yet too often our focus is on the bad guy because he's the one charged with a crime. He's facing prosecution, so he gets the compassion. He gets the lawyer advocating for him in court, on TV, and in the newspapers. He gets the attention of the hand-wringing experts, who want to dissect the process to figure out why the man went from cuddly little baby to rapist or murderer.

I do care about the why—mainly so we can look for ways to head off similar downward spirals in the future. But I'm not interested in the perpetrator's downward spiral to the exclusion of even one ounce of compassion for the victim. That's where I get off the bus. The simple fact is one person has been charged with a crime, and one person has been injured. One person has been charged with committing a terrible act, and the other is in pain as a result. Compassion should go first and foremost to the one in pain.

Unfortunately, it doesn't work this way. In fact, the system is significantly more likely to add to the victim's suffering by refusing her compassion or even acknowledging her status as a victim.

I'm not kidding. In some states, people aren't even allowed to utter the word "victim" in court anymore. A person could be dead as the result of a brutal murder, but the defense will still argue that it's unfair and harmful to the presumption of innocence to call that person a victim.

Think I'm exaggerating? Kobe Bryant's lawyers filed a motion demanding that the court order the prosecutor not to use the word "victim." But it gets worse: A number of defense-friendly types who happened to work at a rape-victim advocacy organization—in Colorado, where the Bryant case was tried—also had a problem with the use of the word "victim" in that case. Some of the staff at the Colorado Coalition Against Sexual Assault quit their jobs in protest over the fact that the organization used the word "victim" when it issued public statements in support of the woman Bryant attacked.

Wow! Someone should have told these people that they did not work at the Colorado Coalition for Defendants' Rights. Anyone who is part of a sexual-assault victims' group is morally obligated to care for victims, irrespective of what the criminal justice system determines. This is not complicated. If you work for an organization that helps victims, you're allowed to call the people you help victims. If you don't like the word, consider going to work at the public defenders' office. And frankly, it doesn't hurt the presumption of innocence to believe a victim is telling the truth even before the criminal justice system renders its verdict unless you're a juror or the judge. People like you and I can think whatever we damn well want to think about the evidence—and we can think a person is guilty even if the jury reaches a not-guilty verdict. Why is this okay? Because we live in the real world where we get to make decisions about things that have nothing to do with the criminal justice process. I will never recommend to any of my friends that they date O. J. Simpson—even though he was acquitted—just as I would never send my kids over for milk and cookies to the home of a child rapist who has been charged—but hasn't yet been convicted. I don't care if he's never convicted. My kids will never be allowed near him. Unfair? Maybe. But while being charged with a crime isn't proof beyond a reasonable doubt, it isn't nothing. A lot of vetting goes on before charges are brought because prosecutors don't like taking on cases they can't win—in fact, it's unethical to do so. This doesn't mean all cases charged are valid and we should not care about the presumption of innocence. It's simply a reminder that the presumption of innocence is a courtroom rule—not a real world mandate—and we can make our own judgments about the people we meet and the information we receive. We'd be fools not to. But we have to be careful not to undermine important constitutional rights. If we're going to judge people harshly in the real world, we have to be very conscientious about rising above personal judgments when we sit in judgment of others as jurors. I'd probably be an especially good juror in a criminal case because I'd be so worried about my own biases, I'd go overboard to compensate. We all have to care about being fair in the courtroom—no matter how we feel about scary people in our personal lives.

If only the defense bar and their ideological allies could understand the importance of being fair. They've got to stop complaining about the word "victim" because victims in the real world need to be validated no matter *what's* going on in court. They can't afford to wait until the criminal justice system gives the okay. Their suffering is real even if the jury says "not guilty." And let's get real: A lot of prejudicial things get said in court during the processing of a criminal case, things far more weighty than the word "victim." You know why? Because that's what happens when you rape, kill, and steal. You put yourself in a situation where people can't help but use harsh language to talk about what you did. The words used to describe criminal behavior are always prejudicial—so is all the evidence—and the word "victim" is no more unfair than the word "witness" (which presumes the person saw something) or "arrest" (which presumes police had probable cause to believe that a crime occurred). I could go on.

Fairness for the accused is important, but let's get off the high horses for a minute. Defense attorneys hate the word "victim," not because it's unfair but because it makes us feel sympathy toward the person who has been harmed—and God forbid we should feel sympathy for someone who was brutalized. Defense attorneys prefer that jurors feel nothing, or better yet, hate the victim. So calling her the accuser or complainant works better because these are mean-sounding words that make a victim seem whiny, or worse, make her seem like the aggressor. Of course, they're both completely incorrect terms. The *government* is the accuser, and the *government* issues the complaint against the accused. The victim is but a witness for the prosecution. But if the defense can succeed at making the jury think the case is between the victim and the perpetrator, then blaming the victim for the crime can create the impression that there's an inverse relationship between the actions of the victim and those of the accused. If a little trouble develops for the victim, the scales necessarily tip in favor of the accused, and presto—reasonable doubt.

This is not at all how things are supposed to work. The fact that the victim has problems is rarely relevant to the issue of guilt, but if the jury winds up hating the victim, the blame game often translates into reasonable doubt because of the power of human drama in the courtroom and because most jurors don't understand how terribly unfair it is to make decisions in criminal cases based on whether they like the victim as a person.

So defense attorneys do whatever they can to generate disgust for the victim. I've seen rape cases where the defense uses rape–shield laws as swords to hurt the victim although such laws are supposed to protect victims by shielding past sexual behavior from disclosure. The fact that defense attorneys can use protective laws to their advantage is a reason to rip these laws out of the books. I may be the only advocate in the country who says this, but I don't care. The simple fact is that rape–shield laws hurt victims way more than they help. Think I'm kidding? Get this: In the Kobe Bryant case, the victim was forced to testify at a pretrial hearing about all sorts of things related to her past sexual conduct. And who forced her to do this, you wonder? The defense did, of course. And why was this allowed to happen? It just so happens that the rape–shield law in Colorado says that a defense attorney has to file a motion in advance of trial if he wants to offer evidence of a victim's past sex life—and that the judge should conduct a hearing to make a determination. The defense argued that if there should be a hearing, then they should have the right to subpoena the victim to the hearing and ask her questions about her sex life. Putting aside the absurdity of a judge allowing the law to be turned on its head this way, the bottom line is that in about a dozen states these types of hearings are allowed, and they are being misused by defense attorneys to conduct outrageous fishing expeditions.

Let me make this clear: If there had been no rape–shield law in Colorado, Bryant's lawyers could never have forced the victim to appear at a hearing and answer questions about her past sex life. And if Bryant had been accused of robbing or beating the victim, rather than raping her, there wouldn't have been a hearing at all because there's no such thing as a robbery–shield law to protect victims from having to answer questions about their prior philanthropy habits. Just rape victims. Just rape–shield laws. It's time to get rid of these laws altogether and ask judges to do their jobs. They all know how to make decisions to determine whether evidence is relevant. It's what they do. There was a time many years ago when judges didn't quite know how to do this with evidence of a woman's sexual past in a rape case. They would make silly rulings like "if she consented in the past, she probably consented on the night in question." So shield laws were enacted to help judges make smarter decisions. Thirty years later, those laws have served their educational purpose and even though some dopey judges will always get it wrong, we don't need any more victims being violated in the name of protection. I like irony as much as the next person, but come on.

Defense attorneys will stop at nothing to create and strengthen an alliance between the public and the perpetrator—including hurting the development of an alliance between the public and the victim. Calling a victim pejorative terms like "accuser" and digging up dirt about her past is all part of the game.

This isn't only an issue for rape victims. The blame game works in any case where the defense can point the finger of responsibility at someone else. This is what happened to Brenda and Damon Van Dam, the parents of seven-year-old Danielle, who was kidnapped from her home and brutally murdered by a disgusting guy named David Westerfield.

Westerfield's attorney, Steven Feldman, the guy I told you about in Chapter 9, knew that he had a vicious animal for a client. The evidence against Westerfield was overwhelming. But rather than just challenging the evidence and making sure his client got a fair trial, he did exactly the thing that makes people hate defense attorneys. He tried to blame Danielle's mother and father for the crime by telling the jury that their lifestyle—they socialized at a local pub, and used intoxicating substances—could have enabled one of their undesirable buddies to steal Danielle from her bed.

If the prosecutor had dared imply that Westerfield was an undesirable type, the defense would have thrown a hissy fit and insisted that the case be dismissed to punish the prosecutor for making derogatory remarks. But the defense could say whatever it damn well pleased about a family that was already heartbroken beyond comprehension, and clearly had nothing to do with the crime. There was not a scintilla of evidence that anyone but Westerfield committed the crime—and yet the defense was allowed to pretend that some unknown boogeyman killed the child and that the parents were responsible because they had an unusual lifestyle.

Our justice system let the defense speculate and theorize irresponsibly about there being a mystery killer and at the same time rub salt in the wounds of people who were in indescribable pain. Maybe you think that mounting a vigorous defense means pulling out all the stops—that there should be no limits to what the defense can say and do. But I don't think you can make the case that the courts have to go along with the cruelest excesses of this approach, including putting victims and their families through legal meat grinders and expect people in pain to smile and put up with it.

The Van Dams could have been as perfect as the Von Trapps in *The Sound of Music*—and it would not have mattered. Westerfield would have kidnapped and murdered little Danielle because he was an evil man, and for no other reason. How the parents lived their private lives was completely irrelevant. But the defense didn't care. The judge didn't care. The parents were violated over and over again, for no reason except that the defense team saw a strategic upside in blaming the victims.

Some jurors are dim enough to let a defense attorney manipulate them into believing that bad parents bear some of the responsibility whenever a child is kidnapped or killed. This is ridiculous, of course, but it makes certain types of jurors feel better about themselves. If they judge the parents harshly, they can psychologically distance themselves from the type of parent whose children get kidnapped and murdered. This makes them feel better about their own lives. It helps them believe that their children will never be kidnapped.

This is not only delusional, it's legally incorrect. The concept of sharing blame is completely inapplicable in the criminal justice system. Unlike a civil suit for money damages—in which one person might be 30 percent responsible, another 40 percent, and so on—in a criminal case, there's no such thing as comparative negligence or shared responsibility. In the criminal justice system, it's an all-or-nothing deal.

In a criminal courtroom, either the bad guy is 100 percent guilty, or not. That's why they have only guilty or not-guilty options. There's no partly guilty option on the verdict form. This holds true for all criminal cases. Why am I thumping away on this point? Because this legal math stuff means that the defense has no right to blame the victim or the victim's parents or anyone else—ever. But they get away with it because it enables them to manipulate jurors' emotions. And, of course, it makes for great courtroom theater. We need to care more about the human costs of this defense strategy.

It seems to me the only time defense attorneys don't try to blame victims and their families is when they think they can get something useful out of them. When Matthew Shepard was brutally beaten to death in 1998 by a group of young men who targeted him because he was gay, the defense didn't suggest the boy might still be alive if his mother had been a better parent by not letting him go out the night he was killed. This is because Shepard's mother, amazingly enough, announced soon after her son's murder that she did not want the prosecutor to seek the death penalty—even though the prosecutor wanted death to be an option for the cowardly killers. The defense not only didn't try to blame Shepard's mother for anything; they actually put her on a pedestal and sang her praises. There was no blame-the-victim nonsense, it was a virtual lovefest, with the defense going on and on about how the victim's mother should be honored and respected.

Of course, if Shepard's mother had said the opposite—that justice in her son's case called for the ultimate punishment—the defense almost certainly would have argued that she was vindictive and acting out of her own feelings of guilt. They would have made the case that victims have no business dictating the punishment in a criminal case because it's the government's responsibility rather than the victim's private lawsuit, and so on.

Using people is always cruel. But blaming victims is worse because it adds insult to injury and because certain victims are more likely to be blamed than others. This means that people who live clean and chaste lives get a better form of justice than those who struggle or who have medical or psychological problems. This just isn't right.

Think of it this way: If blaming victims is acceptable, Rush Limbaugh will have a tough time achieving justice if he's ever victimized by crime. Why? Because the defense will argue his past addiction problems undermine his credibility. Tipper Gore will have trouble, too, because she's suffered from depression. Mel Gibson and Patrick Kennedy won't be treated fairly because they've been to rehab. And forget about Britney Spears if she's ever victimized by violence because she shaved her head and doesn't always wear underwear. She's hopelessly vulnerable to blame-the-victim strategies.

The fact is, all people have weak spots, and criminals take advantage of those weaknesses because they want to get away with their crimes. If we were better at admitting our own faults, we'd be far less likely to blame any victim, ever. This doesn't mean we shouldn't be careful and take steps to protect ourselves and our children from crime. It does mean that if we don't want to reward cowardly criminals, we have to make sure to talk openly and often about how human weaknesses are *vulnerabilities,* not *liabilities.* Take the case of Shawn Hornbeck, the eleven-year-old Missouri boy who was found in 2007 after being kidnapped and held for four years by a man named Michael Devlin. The public was quick to raise an eyebrow about why the child didn't run away. He clearly had lots of opportunities. Devlin let the boy stay home alone and Hornbeck spent time at friends' houses. He even had a cell phone and once reported a stolen bike to the police, but never told anyone he had been kidnapped and never tried to escape. This makes no sense to most people who wonder whether there isn't more to the story. Maybe Hornbeck liked living with Devlin? Maybe Hornbeck was glad to be kidnapped because it got him away from some other problem at home? Another possibility is that he was suffering from what experts call "child sexual abuse accomodation syndrome," a term that describes what terrified kids do when they feel helpless and can't think of a way out of a terrifying situation. Children simply adapt to abuse because they have no choice. In a sense, they normalize what's happening to them because it helps them survive. They don't have the skills, the knowledge, or the maturity to get out of harm's way. Once abuse becomes incorporated into their brains as normal, they don't even think about telling or running away. They essentially give in and accept that being abused is part of life. Is it any wonder that sometimes these kids grow up and abuse others? This behavior makes it hard for jurors to believe children describing protracted abuse because, as rational adults, jurors assume that anyone being abused would either leave or at the very least tell someone. They just don't have the context to understand what looks like very strange behavior. The same kind of unfair harsh judgments get levied against battered women who stay with their violent husbands.

It doesn't really matter whether Shawn Hornbeck was actually experiencing an accomodation syndrome or not because even if the boy ran away from home and begged Devlin to let him stay Devlin had no right to keep the child. Period.

In every case, without exception, not just the cases where we don't like the victim or where we really like the defendant, we simply have to resist the urge to blame victims and their families when crime happens.

If we don't knock it off, defense attorneys will continue to dredge up and sling the mud in the hope that jurors will hate the victim enough to give the bad guy a break. Remember (Wendy) Murphy's Law: The blame game won't work if we don't let it.

SEVENTEEN

Legislating Nothingness and Confusion

WHEN BILL O'REILLY HIRED ME TO WORK WITH HIM on his Jessica's Law initiative to get tough, mandatory punishments for child–sex predators in place in every state, the first thing I did was try to get a handle on what the laws looked like across the country. After a couple of hours, my head was spinning—and this is my field of expertise!

Simply understanding the definitions of child–sex crimes was a struggle. Across our fifty states, there are more than thirty distinct terms to describe the single act of child rape. From "lewd act" to "molestation" to "sexual abuse," we can't even agree on what to call it.

Making laws complicated and incomprehensible is a terrible dirty trick that benefits the perpetrators. Why? Because if the public can't determine from the name of the crime itself what was done to a child, they sure can't figure out whether the punishment fits the crime. If the public can't assess this basic issue, they can't get outraged when injustice happens.

Demystifying all this stuff and getting the public on board to help the laws work better for kids is why Bill O'Reilly started his Jessica's Law campaign in the first place. It hasn't been easy. Not only do lawmakers, judges, and prosecutors hide behind unclear language so that we don't even understand what happened to a child, the laws on sentencing are so complicated that they can make the definitional problems look like a picture of clarity by comparison.

In North Carolina, for example, the law states that the rape of a child under age thirteen carries a mandatory punishment of twelve years in prison. But in another section of the law, judges are given authority to reduce the punishment if they find "extraordinary mitigation." This section is not supposed to apply to rape of a child. But if the prosecutor allows the defendant to plead to a lesser-included offense, the mandatory-sentence law has no applicability. The rapist can get probation, even though that wasn't the intent of the law and it certainly wasn't what the good people in North Carolina expected when they supported their legislature's effort to adopt mandatory-sentencing provisions in their criminal code.

In Washington State, the law that describes the punishment for rape of a child states clearly that the crime carries a mandatory term of five years in prison, but another statute says that this is only a presumptive guideline, not a mandate. Serial rapist and murderer Joseph Duncan was convicted of his first sex offense against a child in Washington in 1980. Inadequate punishment allowed him to roam free and commit more heinous acts against more children in other states. In 2005, Duncan kidnapped and murdered nine-year-old Dylan Groene. Dylan's sister Shasta was also kidnapped but survived. She will no doubt suffer for the rest of her life with the memories of Duncan's brutality. If Washington's laws had been tough enough in 1980, all Duncan's subsequent victims would have been spared unimaginable horror.

In Indiana, the law says that rape of a child carries a mandatory term of twenty years. But twenty actually means ten, because another law states that the sentence is immediately reduced by 50 percent, and with credits for good behavior, the perpetrator can get out even sooner. Who is being held to account for this type of lie being imposed on Indiana's citizens? Answer: no one. The sad thing is—while the innocent public thinks they have tough laws, the child rapists know the deal. They know twenty means ten or less. And they factor this into the cost of doing harm to kids along with an even more disturbing truth: They can usually avoid getting caught altogether by simply threatening to kill the child's mother or pet rabbit. They calculate the odds and, no surprise, they abuse kids over and over again with impunity. Why not? The risk of getting caught is low and even if they do get caught, they can handle a wrist slap. Memo to Indiana lawmakers on behalf of the kids: Thanks a lot.

When I first started looking at the laws, fewer than half of the states had any real mandatory terms of incarceration for child rape. After only one year of his Jessica's Law campaign,

Bill O'Reilly announced that forty states had either passed tough mandatory-sentence laws, or had made a firm commitment to getting the job done.

This is an effort that other news programs should think about as an essential public service. It's scary but true that bad things happen to kids and it's hard to get lawmakers to care because kids don't vote and by and large they don't have any money. In other words, fighting for kids' rights isn't likely to help anyone get elected. Responsible leaders fight for kids anyway. But there aren't enough of them out there.

O'Reilly understands this. As an advocate for kids for twenty years, I understand it, too—very well. I see the duplicitous faces of legislators, especially those who double dip as defense attorneys. They talk a good show about protecting the kids—and then they vote against good laws to protect children because they care more about their private criminal clients than about the needs and wants of their constituents.

It's far too easy for the elected officials to say one thing on the nightly news and then vote the opposite way when a bill like Jessica's Law comes up for a vote. We have to start holding politicians accountable. When a good idea for a new law is proposed, it's got to be filed. And when defense-minded legislators start cutting out sections and adding words, we have to check the proposal carefully to make sure it isn't so full of loopholes and sneaky exceptions that it is useless on the very day it's signed into law.

If we're ever going to hold predators, lawmakers, and officials in the justice system accountable, our sex-crimes laws need to be simplified not murkified (I made that up). And to help the public make sure lawmakers aren't selling us a pig in a poke, the first thing we need to do is make sure all information about sex criminals is publicly available not only on sex-offender registries but on the Internet. When a mother reads about an offender who lives nearby, she needs to know, as soon as possible, more than the fact that a perpetrator was convicted of "molestation." This could mean a one-time pat on a child's rear end, or multiple acts of sodomy. Even classification laws (where an offender is described as being a high risk or a low risk offender according to his dangerousness), don't help much because some states don't have levels, and those that do aren't always getting it right. For example, in Massachusetts, a person can be labeled a level-one offender even if he sodomized a child—which means revealing a person's level isn't nearly enough information to help the public assess a person's dangerousness. Enough details of what each offender did must be made public in every case, so we can figure out exactly what we're dealing with and better protect our children.

And we need to get rid of the confusing language about sex crimes. We need only one phrase: rape of a child. That's it. Why can't all states agree that the word "rape" is the only appropriate and clear way to define an incident involving sexual penetration? This will make it a whole lot easier for officials in Virginia (for example) to figure out what to do with a registered sex offender who just moved there from Alabama. If the only information they have is that the guy was convicted of molestation, they can't make a swift and fair judgment about his dangerousness. And while they're wasting time calling folks in Alabama to find out the details, the guy very likely is making his moves on yet another child.

It would also help if we could enact laws that require a predator's dangerousness to be determined at the time of sentencing, rather than the way we do it now, which is either after the guy is released from prison, or at best, just before. This is absurd. We have a much better chance of making the correct determination about whether a predator is high or low on the dangerousness scale if we look at him close in time to the crime for which he is being incarcerated. Making a decision about dangerousness ten years later, when he's on his way out of prison, is too late to figure out what kinds of conditions should be imposed on the guy during probation or parole. For example, should a guy be fitted with a GPS device? Subjected to drug testing? etc. After a decade behind bars, during which time he was being watched constantly by prison guards, the guy might not seem so dangerous. The determination should be made at the time of sentencing, when the relevant information about his risk to people in the real world is fresh and readily available to decision makers.

This would also be the least expensive way to deal with the issue of dangerousness because the question can be addressed when the relevant facts are also being examined to help the judge figure out the most appropriate punishment overall. In other words, officials will save a ton of money if they double dip determining dangerousness for two purposes at the same time.

Let's air this scenario out a little bit. I'm not saying the perpetrator can't challenge his dangerousness assessment as he nears his release date. He can. But *he* should bear the burden of overcoming the presumptive decision about his dangerousness made at the time of sentencing. When perpetrators realize they have to overcome a presumption of dangerousness, they might actually spend time in prison engaged in meaningful counseling, trying to redeem themselves and earn their way out of being declared dangerous. The current system is backward. It presumes that even the superpredators are safe, and puts the burden on the government to prove dangerousness long after the crime when the perpetrator is about to be released into society. We need to send a strong message to criminals that there's no such thing as an automatic clean slate. They have to earn their way back into civilized society if they ever want to walk free again.

Some will argue that we can't really predict whether someone will commit a crime in the future, and it's true that we can't do it with precision. But remember: These are the same people who said that because the mother of the victim in Michael Jackson's trial lied to receive welfare benefits, the jury should hear about it because (they argued) it meant that she was more inclined to lie in general. They can't have it both ways. Either a person's past behavior does tell us something about their future behavior, or it doesn't. Logically speaking, past behavior can't be a predictor of future behavior only for mothers of crime victims.

In fact, it's far more logical to assume a sex offender will rape again than that a person who lied to welfare officials in the past will make their child lie about sexual abuse in the future. The data show time and again that the average sex offender has dozens and dozens of victims under their belt before they get caught the first time. A large percentage of offenders are simply unstoppable. (I chose that word carefully. I don't want to say incurable, because that would imply that raping children is an illness. It isn't. It's an act of selfish and intentional malice.)

It's impossible to know for sure whether a person will rape or kill again, but we know enough to enable us to take reasonable steps to identify the people that present the greatest risk. This is why it is simply wrong to say that when a sex offender gets out of prison he should bear no burdens on his freedom because he paid his debt to society. This assumes that serving a prison term represents sufficient payment of a debt to society. In fact, as I mentioned earlier, when it comes to hurting kids, the punishment is usually woefully inadequate—the result of a plea bargain rather than a fair assessment of how much incarceration is sufficient to fit the crime.

Even if a particular jerk has paid his debt, it doesn't mean he's safe around kids. I'm not saying that all people with criminal records are unsafe or that people without criminal records are safe. That's clearly not true. But the fact that we can't identify with certainty all the dangerous people is not an excuse not to do the best we can with the perpetrators we know about.

The Constitution promises no person a blank slate after he's been convicted of a horrible crime. Yes, everyone deserves a shot at redemption and forgiveness, but public trust should never be delivered on a silver platter to a convicted sex offender based on the arbitrary passage of time.

We also need the media to do a better job holding elected officials accountable for enacting laws that truly advance the interests of their constituents. The media are pretty good at putting horrible tragedies on the front page—and then doing a follow-up story about how a politician stepped up to the plate to file a new law to prevent future similar tragedies. Unfortunately, there's all too little follow-through after that. The press tends to drop these stories when the deals are being made in secret committees, and power brokers are trading money for a new land deal against the safety of kids. The media rarely shines an antiseptic light on this essential part of the process. They should.

There are exceptions. I'm thinking, for example, about how the *Boston Globe* pounded the Catholic Church about the priest sex-abuse scandal over and over and over again. The result was a reasonably thorough sweeping out of the stable, and a new focus on victims' rights. But when it comes to the widespread abuse of children in the real world, sadly, this type of persistent, dogged coverage is usually missing.

Political leaders take their cues from the media. When the news isn't knocking, they're not talking. Lawmakers jump like new puppies to make things happen when they want to. But if their reelection coffers are being filled by defense attorneys and defense ideologues, and the media isn't on their backs, they're never going to help kids. In short, it's partly the media's fault that we have to wait until some huge tragedy happens to a child before the legislature is shamed into doing something about it.

This is so cruel, isn't it? Waiting for a disaster to happen to a child is too great a price to pay. Would you want it to be your child who paid the price?

When it comes to partisan politics, the fight against sex crimes, even against kids, doesn't fit neatly into one party's platform. Too many conservatives think the government should be out of the business of punishing interpersonal sexual misdeeds and traditional liberals think it's wrong for the state to take away a person's liberty. Even libertarians, as I understand them, don't care enough because they tend to think all government power is bad except to protect national security. No political party is pro rape, of course. And although I'd say the conservatives tend to be a step ahead of the curve on sex crimes, I'd also say that no party is sufficiently pro child, either.

In the absence of political leadership—or the dramatic sacrifice of yet another child—the news media often lack sufficient incentives to talk about the problem. This is why Bill O'Reilly was a bit of a renegade when he took on the task of fighting for tougher laws against sex offenders. Like me, O'Reilly is a nonpartisan who cares more about the issue than someone's political allegiance. So, free from partisan restraint, O'Reilly has supported ideas like GPS tracking devices to better manage the sex offenders who do get out. No, strapping an electronic bracelet on a predator's leg won't stop a guy from finding his next victim. But GPS tracking actually helps a lot because the thing sex offenders tend to worry about most is getting caught and convicted; and they know that with the bracelet on, they'll never be able to say they weren't at the crime scene.

It would also help if every state would get around to eliminating the statute of limitations for child rape. When kids are assaulted, they know it doesn't feel right—but because they haven't reached sexual maturity, they can't understand the nature of the harm they're suffering. Abused kids feel terrorized and they're easily threatened into silence. Because they have no power to do anything about it, they never, ever feel safe in the world. As a result, they develop psychological coping skills that help them not think about the abuse. In the short term, this kind of dissociation from the pain is generally a good thing because it helps abused children deal with their day-to-day reality.

But because of the way the brain works, this is definitely not good for kids in the long run because when child victims become adults, they still have all their suffering inside.

Famed trauma doctor Bessell van der Kolk calls this the Body Keeping Score. In his work looking at the brains of traumatized children, he tracks the way trauma happens and how it stays in the victims' bodies and minds. When kids are old enough to understand the nature of sexual abuse, their brains may have matured sexually, but to heal, they have to fix the brain they had a long time ago, when they were being terrorized. Because that brain doesn't exist anymore, this is not easy.

Many victims never even try to recover. Those that do usually succeed to some extent, but they're never really "cured" of their injuries. It's always in them. Lots turn to drugs and alcohol. Some become abusers themselves. We've never really paid enough attention to these consequences, or how the way abused kids suffer makes reporting and prosecution so difficult.

It can take many years, even a lifetime, for a child to be well enough to deal with abuse. Indeed, the fact that a perpetrator knows there's a statute of limitations makes him more likely to be extra cruel to a child to make sure the victim stays quiet long enough for the clock to run out.

People who complain that eliminating limitation periods altogether would be unconstitutional are either misguided or lying. There's no such thing as a constitutional right to arbitrarily limit the time within which crimes against children have to be prosecuted. That's why they call it a *statute* of limitations: It has nothing to do with the Constitution. It's all about the will of the people. If the public wants the law to provide that the clock should never stop ticking for child rapists, then lawmakers have an obligation to make that happen.

If the accused can't defend himself after a long period of time, he can file a motion to dismiss, explaining why, after so much time, he can't get a fair trial. If the judge agrees, the case is dismissed. But no one can reasonably object to the idea that monsters who pick on kids should spend the rest of their lives looking over their shoulders, wondering if police are behind them. In fact, most cases will never proceed to trial, so making these jerks nervous for a lifetime is the very least we can do.

Finally, let's knock off the complaints about how sex-offender registries are bad for humanity because they stigmatize rapists. Of course they do—that's the point! Society has a right to judge people harshly when they do dastardly things to kids. What, exactly, is so wrong with expecting people who do horrible things to feel bad about and suffer social consequences for their behavior?

Defense attorneys don't seem to mind that victims feel bad or stigmatized. But they want to save the perpetrators from shame and sadness. Stealing for a moment the signature phrase of investigative journalist Dominick Dunne, I find this odd.

Some defense attorneys argue that registries violate sex offenders' privacy rights. I truly don't understand this argument. When a rapist is prosecuted with public dollars in a public courtroom by a public official, it's a public event, period. If a mother of a victim wanted to tell all her friends about what the guy did—or if she wanted to speak about it on television, or write a book—there would be nothing anyone could do to stop her, because there's nothing private about a criminal prosecution. We

could (and should) have C-SPAN-like cameras in every courtroom because prosecution of crime is the quintessential public
concern.

But in virtually every state, when people want to put this
public information in an efficient, accessible, and user-friendly
public place, the ACLU and the criminal defense bar start yelling about privacy rights and how registry laws are bad for humanity. Then these same groups provide political financial
support for legislators in charge of the key committees (with
names like Criminal Justice, Judiciary, and Third Reading) so
that registry laws either don't get passed or become expensive
behemoths that are hard to set up, hard to maintain, and hard to
work with, and then the political hacks can't find the funds in
the budget to maintain the registry. It's an insidious dirty trick—
making good laws useless by making them prohibitively burden-
some and expensive.

In Massachusetts, this sort of nonsense forestalled the en-
actment of a registry law for years. (In fact, we were the last
state in the nation to have one.) We finally got a bill through,
and then the public defenders' office used public tax dollars to
file multiple lawsuits to prevent our registry law from taking
effect.

Unbelievable! In Massachusetts, where we really can't love
our sex offenders enough, is it any wonder we elected Deval
Patrick governor? Patrick described as thoughtful one of our
most notorious rapists—a man named Ben LaGuer who I told
you about earlier. LaGuer brutally raped and assaulted a grandmother in her own home for eight hours and then left her for
dead. Thoughtful? Patrick recommended LaGuer for parole

even though LaGuer persisted in refusing to accept responsibility for his crime or express remorse. If you were a rapist, wouldn't you want to live in Massachusetts?

Obviously, we have a long way to go—and not just in Massachusetts, but all around the country—to get sufficient clarity in the law books and in the minds of our leaders. For now, here's a message to legislators in this country from all of America's children: The bad guys always know when you create confusion and loopholes in laws that help them get away with crime. And believe me, they take advantage of all of them. So knock it off, and try writing clear and truthful laws for a change—laws without tricky exceptions or provisions that you bury in other statutes so that only the lawyers for criminals can find them. Have the guts to make fighting crimes against children easy and affordable for taxpayers. Hold yourselves accountable, for a change; and beware, Bill O'Reilly will be watching to see that you get the job done.

Eighteen

Calling Child Pornography Harmless

When forty-two-year-old David Berglund, a teacher on Cape Cod, was arrested in the fall of 2006 on child pornography charges, the feds announced that they had found more than ten thousand illegal images on his computer.

Don't let your eyes slide over that ten thousand. Recognize that this is an enormous number. Have you ever sent a couple of hundred invitations for a wedding or stuffed five hundred letters in a political campaign? Ten thousand of anything is a lot, and the idea that one person could have so many pictures of little kids being abused seems almost incomprehensible.

But in the world of child pornography, numbers like that

are not uncommon. Exploiting children is the kind of crime that fuels a demand for more, which is why cops rarely find one, or two, or even only a few dozen images on a perpetrator's computer. But this doesn't stop defense attorneys from talking about child pornography as if it's a victimless crime, or some kind of edgy art that's being collected by the defendant as if he's a deep thinker, or at worst some kind of eccentric. "He's not a dangerous pervert," they claim. He's just misunderstood.

Sure he is.

A few of Berglund's photos were described in court as depicting little boys in frontal nudity, lying on beds, and sexually assaulting each other. News reports said other pictures showed children victimized by bondage and whips. But defense attorneys get away with soft-pedaling the stuff. How? Because it's so gruesome that the cops can't get it on TV or in the papers. The public has no way of understanding how horrible this stuff really is. It's the ultimate dirty trick, isn't it? Defense attorneys can claim the pictures aren't that bad, and they get away with lying about it because they know there's no way that police or prosecutors can prove otherwise to the public. In fact, the images can't be shown, and the actions depicted can't even be described in detail, without violating the law.

Bill O'Reilly showcased the Berglund story soon after it broke. He had me and Berglund's lawyer on his show to talk about the story during a special edition of the *O'Reilly Factor* in front of a live audience in Boston in 2006, as part of a Fox News tenth-anniversary special. In my view, O'Reilly deserves an Emmy for the restraint he demonstrated in not punching Berglund's lawyer, Jeffrey Nathan, after Nathan said that ninety days behind bars would be enough punishment because his client didn't hurt any children.

Excuse me? Never mind that Nathan undercut his own client's presumption of innocence by talking about what kind of punishment his client deserved before he had a chance for a trial; let's focus on Nathan's comment about how he didn't see any harm to children. And let's hone in on Nathan's unbelievable claim that it wasn't such a bad crime because the victims were from other countries.

I was sitting right next to the guy when he added that shocker about kids from other countries. I'm glad I didn't have a baseball bat close at hand at that moment, because if I had, I would have been sorely tempted to give Nathan a few whacks upside the head. Bill started yelling at the guy, of course, and my murderous moment passed. But the truly weird thing was that there were actually a few people in the audience who later appeared to be cheering for Nathan, which makes me think that at least some of my fellow residents of Massachusetts are either in the child-porn business or are desperately out of touch with reality.

Maybe some people will never get it. But it's about time that the rest of us started paying attention and standing up for kids because the epidemic of child pornography is seriously out of control. It's destroying the lives of real children. (I don't care where in the world those poor children reside.) And the sexual exploitation of children has been punished on a par with shoplifting for far too long, largely because defense attorneys like Nathan have taken advantage of the fact that most of us have never seen the stuff, which allows them to suggest, falsely, that it's no big deal.

Possession of child pornography isn't even a felony in California and a few other states, including Colorado, Oregon, and North Dakota. It's only a misdemeanor, which means that it gets prosecuted alongside traffic violations and spitting on the sidewalk. But even in a Massachusetts federal court, in a state where possession is a felony, Berglund faced no more than ten years total in prison. Let's do the math. If each image depicts a different child, that's less than a day behind bars for each kid. And even if many pictures show the same child, do we really want to give these types of criminals volume discounts in their punishment for abusing one child over and over again? In effect, the guy gets to commit a lot of crimes for free when he should be getting extra time for participating in repeated abuse of so many defenseless kids.

The Internet has facilitated unprecedented growth, wealth, organizational strength, and even political clout in the child-porn industry in the past few years. Add up all these factors—all moving in the wrong direction—and you can see why the problem is intensifying. Increasingly, bad guys think that they can exploit kids with impunity because, well, most pornographers are getting away with it.

It's outrageous to argue that mere possession doesn't actually hurt children. Of course possession hurts children because without the demand, there would be no industry. Research shows that almost all child rapists use child pornography, either to normalize the behavior for the child or to instruct the victim in how to submit. At the same time, almost all users of child pornography rape and abuse kids. To me, that says that there's obviously a causal connection between possession of photographs and actual child rape. But do we really want to argue over what causes what and to what exact extent one user might become a rapist? Isn't the point that children's lives are at stake? Do we really need to wait until a pile of studies somehow proves scientifically that users of child porn often become child molesters?

Let me answer that for you: No.

In his testimony before Congress in 2002, Michael J. Heimbach—head of the FBI's Crimes Against Children Unit—cited the Hernandez Study (2000). Dr. Andres E. Hernandez, in his capacity as the director of a Federal Sex Offender Treatment Program, found that among federal prisoners who were incarcerated on child-pornography charges, approximately two-thirds had molested children. Even more shocking, the prisoners reported having sexually assaulted an average of more than thirty children each without ever having been detected. And in a study published in the *Journal of Abnormal Psychology* in August 2006, researchers found that using child pornography is a stronger predictor of child–sexual abuse than whether a person was previously convicted of a sexual crime against a child. Think about that. A person who uses child porn is even more dangerous to children than a convicted child rapist!

Can we all just agree, once and for all, that it is unacceptably dangerous to allow users of child pornography to be anywhere near children? And can we also agree that users have to be held just as accountable as child rapists, not only because they represent the demand side but also because the porn industry is set up in such a way that users tend to become producers?

This is literally true. As Attorney General Alberto Gonzales recently explained in testimony to Congress, when users become desensitized to certain photographs, they want something new—more volume, or more violent images. In order to gain access to additional pornography, they have to produce new photos of new kids, thus helping the industry maintain a fresh supply of material, which in turn generates new spending; and the cycle continues.

Against this powerful evidence, some argue that too much government intervention in the fight against child porn threatens First Amendment principles. On the face of it, this is a ridiculous argument. But unless you've actually seen these pictures, you can't really feel that ridiculousness on a gut level. Most of us have no context to visualize a child being raped, which is why I was a bit graphic in the description I included at the outset of this chapter. We need to understand how awful this stuff really is, and believe me, the abuse I described doesn't begin to scratch the surface.

Let's put the silly art claim to rest once and for all. Child pornography is never an airbrushed photo of a little boy on the beach with his rear end showing. Never. According to a 2005 study funded by Congress, 80 percent of child pornography depicts children being penetrated. This is what you would think of as rape and sodomy. A full 21 percent also involved sadism such as bondage, whips, chains, and ligatures wrapped around little arms, legs, and necks while body parts and objects are inserted into tiny private areas. Something like 83 percent of child pornography depicts children between ages six and twelve and only 1 percent consists of images of simple child nudity—the stuff some people claim is art. Sadly and maybe most disturbing, according to Attorney General Gonzales, it's often parents taking the pictures—as we saw with Justin Berry, the handsome young man who testified before Congress in 2006 about being pimped by his father while he engaged in sex acts for money via a Webcam from his home.

Justin Berry's story brought tough, cynical old congressmen to tears. Most of them hadn't heard of anything quite so shocking before. Well, this level of ignorance is itself shocking because at any given moment, more than fifty thousand people are lurking on the Internet, hunting for children they can exploit and rape for profit. Members of Congress, who supposedly are bright people with strong connections to reality, should not have been so surprised, but the fact that they were is strong evidence that we have a lot of work to do.

Child pornography is a multibillion-dollar business run by people who are destroying innocent children's lives for money. They know that law enforcement will never have enough resources to stop them completely. This is why we need more public/private partnerships, like NBC's "To Catch a Predator" program. The wealth of a major network helps stretch law enforcement's budget. But money alone will never do the trick because pornographers know the ACLU and others will spend another ton of money defending kiddie porn by waving the flag around.

The ACLU has done some very important work, especially when it comes to protecting subversive political speech. But while they will try to persuade you that their advocacy and support for the porn business is not an endorsement of child sexual abuse or "real" (as opposed to "virtual") child pornography, consider that the former president of the Virginia chapter of the ACLU was arrested in 2007 on child porn charges. According to a criminal complaint against him, Charles Rust Tierney allegedly subscribed to hard-core child porn Web sites over a period of years. This is a guy who successfully fought on behalf of the ACLU to ensure that the computers in Virginia's public libraries would not have filters to prevent access to child pornography. ACLU chapters around the country have also:

1) Filed lawsuits opposing sex offender registries.
2) Challenged laws that require sex predators to stay away from schools, parks, day care centers, and libraries.
3) Opposed mandatory minimum sentences for child rapists.
4) Provided free legal services to NAMBLA in a lawsuit brought by the family of a murdered ten-year-old boy whose killers reportedly collected the group's literature and viewed its Web site shortly before the crime. NAMBLA has advocated the abolition of laws that make it a crime for adults to have sex with children.
5) Argued in court that the rape of a fourteen-year-old boy was not a crime, in part because teenagers have a constitutional right to be "free from state compulsion" when making personal decisions about sexual activity.

Here's my prescription for the ACLU: Take a vacation from protecting pornographers for a while, and fight to protect children's freedoms for a change. Even the densest member of the

ACLU can understand the downside of slavery, and that's exactly what child pornography is: It's using kids as sex slaves for profit. Someone needs to tell the ACLU we have much more to fear from these private businessmen than from the government power that hopefully, one day, will bring them down.

In the meantime, we can all help protect kids by noticing the warning signs before the harm happens. When the Mark Foley scandal broke in 2006 his congressional colleagues were falling all over themselves trying to explain why certain information in an e-mail wasn't explicit enough to prove that Foley was truly dangerous. But the red flags had been flying over Foley's inappropriate behavior with congressional pages for a long time—well before the guy was bold and stupid enough to put his intentions in writing.

Most pedo-perps are too smart to put anything in writing, which is why parents, congressmen, and anyone else who's responsible for the well-being of children have a duty to learn what red flags look like, so they can intervene before a situation gets out of control.

Like what, for example? Child pornographers and perpetrators who prey on kids often display an unusual interest in young people. They usually have only a few close friends of their own age. Pedo-perps are typically narcissistic and naive, often behaving in ways that disrespect boundaries in interpersonal relationships.

Pedo-perps are not typically gay. Most child–sex offenses are male-on-female, although some offenders are homosexual in orientation. (I mentioned earlier the loathsome NAMBLA, which exists especially for such offenders.) In such cases, of course, the offender expresses a special interest in boys. But it's not about homosexuals running amok. For the most part, even homosexual child pornography has nothing to do with gay feelings. Don't let people like Mark Foley (who tried to win sympathy points by announcing he was gay when his scandal hit) blow smoke by telling you otherwise.

As renowned expert Dr. Anna Salter writes in her book, *Predators,* pedo-perps typically groom their victims and test the waters. They use inappropriate language or touch a child's leg to see how a potential victim reacts. If the child doesn't protest, the behavior is very likely to escalate. When a child is effectively groomed, the perpetrator has a much easier time causing the child to submit to sexual contact, which is why it is critical for parents to recognize the symptoms of grooming behavior at the earliest possible stage.

To ensure a child doesn't tell, a pedo-perp might include illicit behavior in the grooming process; for example, showing a kid pornography, or giving him alcohol or drugs. For pubescent teenagers, access to illicit material can be exciting, yet because they know their parents will disapprove, they keep it a secret. Then when the pornography or sexual abuse starts happening, the child feels he cannot tell anyone because he's done something bad and will get into trouble.

Not all perpetrators groom their victims, and not all kids show signs that they're being harmed. Sometimes a child really likes the extra attention—even though he or she hates the abuse—especially when the attention is coming from someone important. Kids get confused about feeling good and bad at the same time, so they stay quiet. Again, they feel partly responsible as if they deserved the abuse or somehow owed the perp a little sex in exchange for all the attention, favorable treatment, and access to illicit goodies.

Child abusers are easy to spot as long as the people responsible for protecting kids know what they're looking for. All too often, though, special attention from a relative or other trusted adult goes unnoticed because it seems like an expression of generosity and kindness. And of course, sometimes it is. But until we start questioning whether an adult's behavior around a child might be too good to be true, the pornographers and pedo-perps will continue to prey on children, undetected.

Fixing this problem is all about keeping the forest in sight, even as you're looking at the trees. Yes, we have to scrutinize the language in an e-mail to see whether the content indicates that a child is in danger. But if we're waiting for the smoking gun or only looking at e-mails, we're going to keep failing the kids.

Finally, we have to be honest with ourselves and, as scary as it is, accept the harsh reality of what's happening to our children. Turning a blind eye to the warning signs usually feels a whole lot better than allowing ourselves to think the worst of a situation. After all: What parent wants to believe that their child is being sexually abused or exploited? But this head-in-the-sand approach is terribly dangerous to kids so we have to give up a little bit of our desire to believe that our children are safe.

If we don't, people who prey on kids will continue to do

what they do while we sit in denial—seeing the smoke but taking no action because there doesn't seem to be any fire.

This obviously didn't work to protect children in Foley's case, and it will never work for any child. As we've seen in far too many cases, by the time the smoke becomes a fire, too many kids will have been burned.

NINETEEN

Inventing Imaginary Constitutional Rights

WE'VE ALL HEARD OF MIRANDA WARNINGS, AND THE so-called Miranda rights that grow out of them. They're very important. But not every violation requires the beheading of a police officer or the release of a murderer from prison. Try telling that to those defense attorneys who can't stop themselves from claiming that everything that police do wrong—whether intentionally or by mistake, whether a major or a minor infraction—requires the most severe sanctions against the cops and complete freedom for the criminal.

Miranda rights weren't even technically constitutional rights until a few years ago. In 1966, the Supreme Court ruled in the Miranda case that police had to warn criminal suspects in their custody that they had the right to remain silent. This was, and is, critically important because under the Fifth Amendment to the Constitution, no one should be coerced by the state to become a witness against himself. In a free society, the government absolutely must obtain its evidence in a way that shows the utmost respect for the integrity and value of civil liberties. Still, the decision to require cops to give Miranda warnings was not a constitutional mandate—it was an idea, created by the court, designed to give force to the right of all suspects to remain silent. The Supreme Court suggested that Congress could enact legislation to propose a different way of protecting Fifth Amendment rights, which they subsequently did, and so it was clear that if police did not read suspects their rights, it was not necessarily a constitutional violation—and it certainly wasn't as serious an infraction as, say, a violation of due process or the Fourth Amendment right against unreasonable searches and seizures.

Our founding fathers wanted to ensure that we'd never have a legal system that would let cops torture a suspect into confessing—and this cannot be overstated. Even if cops are certain a guy is guilty, coercing a confession is unacceptable. It's not only that we prefer only truthful confessions but also that we like the law to maintain healthy restraints on law enforcement. In other words, Miranda rights help to maintain a fair balance of power between the government and the individual. This is all good stuff.

But when every Miranda violation, no matter how slight, becomes the means by which defense attorneys demand the most extreme remedies, such as dismissal of criminal charges and lawsuits against cops, we're all in deep trouble.

Just as wrapping child pornography in the flag demeans the First Amendment, using technical Miranda violations to insist that murder charges be dismissed does not track with the intent of the Fifth Amendment, and it diminishes the seriousness of other more extreme violations of constitutional rights.

But this is exactly what some defense attorneys were clamoring for in early 2006 when the judge in Florida handling the prosecution of John Couey for the brutal rape and murder of little Jessica Lunsford threw out Couey's confession on the grounds it was obtained in violation of his Miranda rights.

The simplest way to state the legal issue is that the confession was excluded because police did not stop questioning the suspect after he indicated that he wanted a lawyer. Most observers, like me, said things like, "Well, the judge was correct, but it's okay, because there's plenty of evidence left over to prove guilt." A bunch of defense attorneys, however, said the Constitution demands that all the evidence—including the discovery of little Jessica's body, hugging a stuffed animal, and buried in the killer's backyard—should have been excluded, and the whole case should have been dismissed to punish the cops for their terrible behavior.

I want to make sure you're getting this. Some defense attorneys actually argued that not only should self-incriminating statements obtained incorrectly be suppressed, which is entirely appropriate, but a confessed child murderer should get a total pass to teach the cops a lesson and protect liberty for all of us.

Releasing John Couey from prison will keep us free?

I understand the benefits to liberty when police are punished for misdeeds. If they refuse to read a guy his rights—or if they whack him on the spine with a phone book to make him confess—they deserve to be made an example of, both to strengthen our civil rights and to deter the next law-enforcement official who might be tempted to go over the line. But these things didn't happen in the Lunsford case. Not even close. In the Lunsford case, not only was there no torture, there wasn't even force or coercion. The killer was not threatened in order to make him confess—and in light of his extensive criminal record, you can bet he was well aware of his Miranda rights. But the police read them to him anyway, more than once.

After being told he had the right to remain silent and to speak with an attorney, he sang like a bird, mostly about things unrelated to Jessica Lunsford. When police got to the subject of the child's murder, they mentioned using a polygraph, and the killer's chatty personality turned chilly—something that experienced detectives know often indicates consciousness of guilt. Then the suspect made several references to an attorney, and the police asked him to confirm that he only wanted an attorney for the polygraph portion of the interrogation. They specifically asked whether it was okay for the verbal interrogation to continue, and the suspect was less than clear about whether he wanted to stop talking. Indeed, he not only kept talking, he soon confessed in detail to the brutal rape and murder of little Jessica.

If a suspect says he wants a lawyer, police should stop the interrogation. But if the request is unclear ("I wonder if I should call a lawyer"), police can and should take advantage of the equivocation. This is what the cops tried to do in the Lunsford case. They took advantage of the guy's indecisiveness and tried to persuade him that he only wanted a lawyer for the lie-detector test.

So the guy was an idiot. He fell for it. The Constitution says nothing about police not taking advantage of idiot murderers.

Nevertheless, the judge ruled that the police should have stopped asking questions at that point and because of this, the killer's confession was tossed. Fortunately, the remaining evidence—including DNA, the child's body, and a jailhouse confession—was not suppressed and was sufficient to prove guilt. Couey was convicted and sentenced to death in 2007. Still, criticism abounds from the defense bar, whose most radical members bemoan the fact that the case was not dismissed in its entirety.

This extreme position makes a mockery out of the Constitution because it assumes that all Miranda violations cause the same harm to the rights of the individual. In other words, when police persist in asking questions after an unclear Miranda waiver, it is no different from when they whack someone on the head to force a confession. This is, of course, ridiculous. Not all mistakes that affect Miranda rights demand the same remedy, which is why dismissing the entire Lunsford case would have been wrong. The judge obviously understood that the Constitution never requires dismissal of a serious criminal case when to do so would produce no constitutional benefit.

Yes, Miranda rights are important. But just as a punishment should be proportionate to the crime, sanctions against police should be proportionate to the violation.

———

Some defense attorneys think that as long as their client stands charged with a crime, anything they want to do—every motion they file, every step they take—is somehow connected to a constitutional right, and everything bad that happens to a defendant is a threat to civil liberties.

Not true by a long shot. But this view of the Constitution is an increasingly common sentiment among the defense bar, and someone has to put the brakes on. Remember while one part of the Constitution is being misapplied to the benefit of child killers, another section, the First Amendment, is facilitating the unfair treatment of victims.

Who can forget that during the Kobe Bryant trial, the airwaves were full of utter nonsense about the victim? Defense pundits were only too happy to analyze how all the dirt about the victim would help the defense win the case because the jury would think unfair things about her, even if the dirt was false or had nothing to do with the trial. What I want to know is where is it written that the defense has a constitutional right to taint the jury pool with harmful information about an innocent citizen? The answer is: There isn't one. Yet we have defense attorneys citing the First Amendment as a justification to lie about crime victims.

The framers would not be pleased.

The media should help out here and treat victims exactly the way it treats defendants when it comes to restraining the dissemination of prejudicial evidence. In the courtroom, defendants do have a superior constitutional status compared to the status of the victim, but when it comes to using the media to influence the potential jurors, the accused and the victim stand on equal footing, which means that if defense attorneys are going to dump dirt about the victim, then prosecutors should be allowed to dump dirt about the perpetrator. And if defense attorneys are going to celebrate the fact that the jury hears irrelevant or false information about the victim, then victim attorneys are going to celebrate the fact that the jury hears unfair or suppressed evidence about the accused.

One could argue that the media should provide *extra* protection to victims by refusing to print any prejudicial information until a judge makes a decision on admissibility, which will ordinarily be at the time of trial. The judge can then order the jury not to read the newspapers or watch TV news as a way of protecting the integrity of the trial process and the privacy rights of victims. I can't argue for the same level of nondisclosure of evidence against the accused because some information needs to be disclosed after the government decides to bring charges against a person. Media oversight ensures that the prosecutor is not abusing his or her power and promotes public safety by letting us know who has been charged with a serious crime. These concerns do not apply to victims.

This doesn't mean defendants won't get a fair shake. It only means victims won't get an unfair shake. Judges can and should always make sure that jurors chosen for a criminal trial make a sincere promise to render a verdict based only on the evidence they hear during trial, without regard for what they read or heard about on the news.

But defense attorneys have to do their part, too, by resisting the urge to insist that everything that happens to a criminal is a violation of, and all the bad things that happen to victims are authorized by, the Constitution.

For example, defense attorney often argue that it violates the accused's constitutional rights for a police officer to wear his uniform during trial. Why? Because the jury will be biased in favor of a man in uniform. But if a defense attorney is representing a priest accused of child rape, he gets indignant at the idea that the priest shouldn't be allowed to wear his collar in court. Why? Because he has a constitutional right to practice his religion during his testimony. Oh, please! The Constitution has nothing to do with any of this.

I can only guess what's next. Demanding that a case be dismissed to punish a prosecutor for smiling at a child victim during trial? Forbidding use of the word "rape" during a rape trial? Insisting that the Constitution allows a rapist to inspect a victim's bedroom closet to look for evidence?

When the law and the media set no boundaries and defense attorneys claim to see constitutional rights around every corner, who's to blame when things get out of control? The defense attorney who takes advantage of the fact that nobody's reining him in—or the rest of us who stay silent when we should be marching in the streets?

Twenty

Launching Political Persecutions

I HOPE THAT BY NOW YOU'VE PICKED UP ON A THEME, hardly hidden and unapologetically injected into many chapters of this book: I'm as mean as it gets when it comes to criminals.

I'm sick of hearing how punishment is vengeance, imprisonment does no good, and all the rest of the addle-brained nonsense that emerges—sometimes from judges on the bench, and frequently on the front steps of courthouses, with cameras rolling as some tree-hugging defense attorney whines that jails are bad, punishment is fascism, blah, blah, blah.

Punishment works. That's why when judges go soft on the bad guys out of some twisted allegiance to the idea that thugs need hugs, my arms start flailing, and I get really steamed. When someone tries to defend their position by adding something stupid like, "We don't have enough prison space to lock up all the child predators," I'm ready to tear my hair out. If we really don't have room to lock up the dangerous criminals, what the hell were we doing wasting a bed on Martha Stewart?

I know she lied, and lying is wrong, whether it's to a neighbor, a judge, or an SEC investigator. But federal prosecutors who went after Martha Stewart spent way too much of the public's money sending a liar to prison. Suppose there had been only one bed left for a female criminal. Who would you rather see in it? Martha, or one of the umpteen teachers who have perpetrated sex crimes against their students in the past couple of years— teachers who rarely saw a single day, much less nine months, behind bars?

What do we really accomplish by sending a slick businesswoman to jail, anyway?

I realize it's important to send a message, even with nonviolent crime, when the goal is to prevent similar misconduct in the future. But didn't Martha get that message, early and loud, when she was forced to resign from her company, taking a huge financial hit, and was then indicted on the world stage? Sure, pounding a criminal a little extra sometimes makes sense, if you're trying to set an example for others. But this agenda can be carried too far. When prosecutors go overboard—demanding incarceration and making a small case seem like the most important prosecution since the Scopes Trial—the backlash can nullify the intended message. Or worse, as in Stewart's case, it can breed cynicism and contempt for the entire justice system. How long can you keep believing in a system that can't seem to get its priorities straight?

It was clear from the beginning why the feds latched on to Martha Stewart: Prosecutors get a lot of public attention when they go after a celebrity. As sending a message goes, the feds get a lot of bang for their (taxpayer) bucks when millions of people are wrapped up in watching a prosecution unfold. Will she go to jail, or won't she?

By whacking around a big cheese like Stewart, the feds were attempting to give us renewed confidence in the integrity of the stock market. They were trying to reassure us that our stocks were safe—and that future investments were a good idea—because prosecutors were finally getting tough on corporate criminals.

But let's be honest: There never would have been a prosecution if Martha Stewart was viewed by the public as some sort of secular saint. Take Kelly Ripa, for example. Suppose Kelly had gotten the same stock tip from Martha's friend and tipster Sam Waksal and saved a bundle of money as a result. She could have invited Waksal onto her show and thanked him publicly for the heads-up about the impending implosion of Waksal's company, and there'd have been no prosecution. The same goes for Bill Cosby, Julie Andrews, and anyone who even looks a little bit like Jimmy Stewart. Our secular saints are held harmless. The feds would have raised a wet finger to the wind, concluded that angry mobs of fans in the streets would have been bad for public relations—not to mention for the outcome of the next presidential election from an incumbent's point of view—and the higher-ups would have put the kibosh on prosecution. Sure, there might have been a fine, a hand slap, community service, and so on; but there would have been no protracted prosecution, and certainly no politically unpalatable prison time.

But prosecutors could easily get away with an over-the-top prosecution of a "bitchy" woman who made it big in a man's world. Why? Because when the wet finger gets raised on a mean character like Martha Stewart, the wind doesn't blow. There's no political downside to going after a hugely successful business-woman with a reputation for behaving badly and apologizing to nobody on her way up the ladder of success. The prosecutors knew they could use Martha as a whipping girl simply because she was disliked by enough people. Forget that other CEOs who had ruined lives and decimated retirement funds were still walk-ing the streets. People would pay attention to and applaud the Martha Show.

But there's some evidence that the public saw right through this strategy. Opinion makers asked about the proportionality of the case: Why go after Martha but not bigger fish? The stock price of Martha's own company sagged but then recov-ered. People, especially women's groups, rallied around her. Instead of successfully exploiting Stewart based on her gender (there's no doubt gender had something to do with it), the prosecution, ironically enough, just may have helped revive the feminist movement.

Politically motivated, prosecutorial decision making is not new. But when justice is served up on a platter of prejudice, it hurts the system. And this matters a lot, especially when the whole country is watching.

We need to do two things to make sure this type of prosecu-tion doesn't happen again. First, we need to make it up to

Martha, somehow. And second, we need to send the feds a strong message about our disgust for the way they did business in her case.

How should we make it up to Martha? For my part, I'm buying up Martha Stewart table linens and other kitchen stuff although I have absolutely no need for any of it. I'm even buying her magazine—although again, I have no intention of cooking a gourmet meal or growing a new variety of daisies or building a trellis to serve as a dramatic-but-tasteful backdrop for my garden. (I'm not even sure that my few scraggly perennials count as a garden.)

I'm not complaining about all this because I'm a woman. I actually know a lot of men who feel the same way that I do. In fact, I know a lot of men who are better advocates for women than some women's-rights groups. The simple truth is it doesn't matter what kind of body parts you have if you care about things like unfair prosecutions. So you don't have to be a Martha Stewart fan to want to get a message to the feds about their decision to incarcerate her for nine months. Martha's been out of prison for a while, so it doesn't make sense to complain about her case anymore, but here's one thing you can do if they try it again on someone else. Write a letter to both of your senators and to your representative in the House, and say, "I'm shocked that the government wasted my tax dollars. All my friends agree with me and we intend to vote in the next election based on what you do about this issue."

Once again: I'm not saying that Stewart is innocent. There's no question she violated the law, and for that she had to pay a price. But people need to be punished for what they do—not who they are—and the punishment should be proportionate, not gratuitous. Martha Stewart should have paid a fine, period.

And by the way: The fact that a prosecution is popular doesn't make it just. Think of the Salem Witch Trials. Egged on by an anxious public that saw witches behind every bush, the authorities in Salem, Massachusetts, rounded up a bunch of people (mainly, but not exclusively, women), then prosecuted them, and ultimately executed twenty of them, to the general approval of the populace.

Couldn't happen today, right? Don't count on it. The fact is: Prosecutors have a ton of power, and we the public have very few options for holding them accountable when they abuse their authority. As I suggested earlier, when it's a state prosecutor, you can work with others to prevent the reelection of a bad district attorney. But federal prosecutors, known as United States Attorneys, are appointed, not elected, which means you have to think about who you are voting for in the presidential and congressional races in your district to have any effect on the appointment of a federal prosecutor.

We need new ideas, though, because the political response isn't really adequate even for state prosecutors. For one thing, it just doesn't work fast enough to deal with a dangerously bad prosecutor. We can't afford to let someone who is causing injustices stay in office for four years while we wait for a chance to vote for someone different. Someone different might not even run the next time around. So we need a way of influencing prosecutors' decisions while they are in office to prevent them from overdoing it, as with Martha Stewart, or underdoing it, as with so many district artorneys, who mishandle cases against child predators.

Court-watch programs are a good idea, whereby citizens agree to volunteer their time literally to sit in court and take notes to record the prosecutor's actions. This information then gets logged into a database and ultimately reported to the public on a regular basis. These types of public oversight groups can help inform the public about things like the deals that prosecutors are making on certain cases and what percentage of tax dollars is being spent on what types of prosecutions. If plea bargains are being doled out like candy and expenditures are out of balance, at least the public will hear about it. And who knows? They might launch a protest at the DA's office, or undertake a letter-writing campaign to the local media. The point is that the public would at least know what is going on—a great improvement over the situation we have today.

With better information about how our tax dollars are being spent to fight crime, we can work together to make sure the good prosecutors get in and the bad ones lose their jobs in a tide of public humiliation.

At the end of the day, it's not only about politics; it's about each of us making sure the ultimate government power is used responsibly to serve the public interest—and not as theater for a prosecutor's political agenda. It's worth thinking about how we might respond to the next political persecution, because this time it was Martha Stewart—but next time it might be someone like you.

TWENTY-ONE

Suing the Victim

IN 2005 CYLE JONES WAS CONVICTED OF SEXUALLY assaulting another student at the Groton-Dunstable High School in Massachusetts. After the criminal case was over, Jones's lawyer, Nelson P. Lovins, filed a suit against the victim and her mother, claiming they violated Jones's civil rights. The suit argued that the victim's family should pay Jones money damages because they caused him emotional distress. How did a victim and her mother cause a perpetrator emotional distress, you wonder. By reporting the crime to police and speaking publicly about the assault. I'm not kidding. The lawsuit was eventually thrown out and the lawyer was punished for bringing an unjust lawsuit, but can you believe the audacity of this sex offender and his attorney?

Does this make you crazy? It makes me crazy.

How about another example in the same vein? A bunch of parents in the town of Norfolk, Massachusetts, were sued in 2006 when they protested the decision to allow four convicted sex offenders to live in a group home only steps from families with small children. Parents in the neighborhood were terrified. They made the point, loudly, that this particular group home was supposed to house people with disabilities—not criminals, and certainly not convicted sex offenders. After much public outcry, the owner of the property moved the four sex offenders to another location. The families were thrilled that their children would be safe.

Happy ending, right? Wrong. The parents' happiness was short-lived because they soon found themselves the targets of a vicious lawsuit, filed by David J. Apfel and Alisha R. Bloom of the noted Boston law firm Goodwin Procter LLP. These lawyers said that the families violated the criminals' rights by complaining about dangerous sex offenders living in the neighborhood.

The sex offenders in both cases claimed they suffered from mental problems, and that as people with psychological issues, they were entitled to special rights under the Americans with Disabilities Act. It was a stunning assertion. (It still stuns me as I write about it today.) These guys literally demanded the same kind of special protections accorded black citizens under civil rights law; that is, protections designed to redress unfair prejudice.

Give me a break. It's not unfair to discriminate against convicted sex offenders. In fact, it is essential to heap public scorn and loathing on people who commit sex crimes against children. And whether or not you agree with me that these types of offenders should never walk around free in society, I hope you'll agree they hardly deserve extra protection, in the form of civil rights laws, to protect them from discrimination.

Defending sex offenders to make sure that they get a fair trial is a necessary, even honorable thing to do. What's not honorable is hurting innocent citizens and victims by suing them for reporting crime to police or exercising their own constitutional rights of free speech. Lawyers who file lawsuits against victims are one reason why people have so much disdain for defense attorneys. If it stopped there, maybe that wouldn't be such a bad thing. But when people lose faith in lawyers—the professionals who stand as representatives of the system—it's only a short step to losing faith in law altogether. And when people lose faith in the system as a whole, they either check out, refusing to lend a hand when they're needed as jurors or witnesses, or worse, they take matters into their own hands by becoming vigilantes.

Judging from the e-mails and letters that I receive, the public is clearly getting fed up with lawyers who cater excessively to criminals. Even lawyers themselves are at the end of their rope. In 2006, Jonathan Edington, a Connecticut attorney, killed his neighbor Barry James after Edington's wife told him that James had molested their two-year-old daughter.

As it turned out the child had not been molested, but still, an awful lot of people sympathize with Edington because they believe they would have felt the same rage if they had been told their child had been molested. No, Edington doesn't deserve a pass and, frankly, James's family can and should sue Edington for causing James's death because nobody deserves to die, and taking the law into your own hands is always wrong. But what should we conclude when a lawyer becomes a vigilante? Is this just the isolated act of a parent deranged by grief? Or is there some sort of judgment here about the efficacy and fairness of the system, too?

Vigilantism is wrong, period. But on the off chance that a sex offender is reading these pages, I have a word of advice for you: Beware. True, something like 90 percent of child–sex crimes are never reported, which is pretty good odds for rapists who pick on kids. But anecdotal evidence suggests that when a child does tell someone, the chances are increasing that offenders will pay a serious price, maybe even the ultimate price, by an angry public that is sick and tired of waiting around for the justice system to get the job done. We've all heard the stories about how prison inmates are particularly rough on fellow prisoners who have abused children. It isn't right but it's the kind of canary-in-a-coal-mine evidence that suggests the public is very dissatisfied with the status quo.

Lawyers for sex offenders should take a lesson and stop fueling the fire in the belly of a furious public by filing crazy lawsuits. Society is clearly at the end of its rope if people accused of molesting kids, even incorrectly, are getting killed—by lawyers. Filing lawsuits against innocent victims and protective parents is surely a move that will expose even more of their pedo-perp clients to harm. It's bad enough the justice system doesn't come close to dealing responsibly with sex offenders.

Now parents and victims have to worry about getting sued on the theory that these perps deserve special legal protections because they're sick?

Rapists aren't sick; they're criminals. Period. And in fact, claiming to be sick is giving the truly mentally ill a bad name. Child predators deserve to be stigmatized and shamed—some even condemned for the rest of their lives—for choosing kids as their victims. Nothing less will do. Nothing less will protect our kids.

Perpetrating sexual violence truly is a choice for sex offenders, even if it is a choice that's driven by a compulsion. Don't be tricked into thinking otherwise. Lots of people have urges, and lots of those urges are bad ones. But most of the time, they don't act on them when that would mean hurting someone else, especially a child. And when they do act on their urges, we don't (or shouldn't) say, "Oh, that's okay; don't worry about it; you have a mental illness." Instead, we say (or we should say), "You had a choice, and you chose to indulge yourself rather than restrain yourself. For that, you have to be punished."

Too many people wrongfully believe that criminal sexual abuse occurs because the perpetrator couldn't help himself. But if that were true, wouldn't people be doing all sorts of horrible things in public every day without regard for consequences? Couldn't we all say our bad behavior, whatever form it took, was the result of some type of compulsive mental illness? There's no stronger compulsion than the need to use the bathroom; and yet it's pretty damn rare for someone to just pull his or her pants down and use the middle of Main Street as a toilet. If people can control their bathroom needs, they can certainly control their impulse to rape children. And if they can't, they need to be put away.

Today, we have more experts involved in court cases (usually at taxpayer expense) supporting sex offenders than comforting victimized kids. Is this twisted, or what? Who deserves the comfort—the rapist, or the rapist's victim? Whose psychological well-being should we be more worried about—that of a convicted criminal who will feel sad if he can't get a reduced prison sentence or live in a group home near kids, or that of a child's mother who won't sleep a wink so long as four sex offenders live across the street? Who deserves to get sued—the rapist for committing his crime, or the victim for talking about it publicly?

Is it any wonder so many people truly hate defense lawyers?

The good news is: Citizens are fighting back. They are not only successfully defending themselves, they are winning money damages to compensate them for the pain and expense of having to deal with ridiculous, misguided, and cruel lawsuits. One clever trick victims are using to protect their free speech and protest rights is the filing of motions to dismiss lawsuits on the ground that they violate innocent citizens' rights when sex offenders sue them for exercising their constitutional freedoms.

Let me explain. In many states, under so-called anti-SLAPP (Strategic Litigation Against Public Participation) laws, citizens are granted immunity from lawsuits when they engage in public-participation activities such as testifying in court or speaking publicly about crime. Anti-SLAPP laws protect the rights of all citizens to speak openly about matters such as the conduct of sex offenders, and to protest loudly when dangerous predators move into a neighborhood filled with children.

Unfortunately, not enough citizens and victims know about their rights under anti-SLAPP laws, because these laws are a relatively recent innovation, and because they weren't expressly designed to help victims of violence. They were initially crafted to give homeowners protection against lawsuits when they were sued for protesting things like having toxic chemicals dumped in a local playground. The chemical company would sue the protesters for libel and slander and offer to settle the case if the homeowners stopped protesting. Anti-SLAPP laws allow the homeowner to punish the company for filing the lawsuit.

I immediately recognized the benefits of this type of law to victims because I had seen similar lawsuits for libel and slander lodged by defense attorneys against victims who had reported crimes to police and testified about the crime in a public courtroom. I'm told that I was the first lawyer in the country to use an anti-SLAPP law on behalf of a battered woman, more than a decade ago, to dismiss a lawsuit that had been filed against her by her husband after he was convicted of abusing her. Today, lots of advocates for victims use anti-SLAPP laws. But we need to spread the word because too many law-abiding citizens simply crumble in fear and give up their rights when a process server shows up at their door and hands them papers saying they're being sued for ten million dollars.

Crime victims need to know that anti-SLAPP laws are very easy to use, and are highly effective. If a victim or wins her anti-SLAPP motion, the lawyer who filed the suit is mandated to pay her attorney's fee and other costs. Make no mistake about it: When lawyers who sue victims have to pay fines, they stop suing victims.

The American Civil Liberties Union (ACLU) often uses anti-SLAPP laws to defend, for free, people who are sued for exercising their free speech and protest rights. Unfortunately, but perhaps not surprisingly, the ACLU in some states, including Massachusetts, draws a line at representing crime victims or parents trying to protect their children from sex predators. If you get the chance, ask someone at the ACLU someday why this is so. Let me know what they say to try to justify this particular hypocrisy.

I suspect the answer will reveal at least one truth about the ACLU: that they just can't seem to accept the idea that the Constitution belongs to everyone—not just accused criminals. Until they get this straight, we need not only anti-SLAPP laws but also a privately funded ICLU (Innocent Citizens' Liberties Union) to protect the fundamental rights of victims and innocent people everywhere to speak out—loudly and often—whenever crime occurs or public safety is threatened.

If we work together, lawsuits against victims and parents will stop overnight—I guarantee it. Remember the new (Wendy) Murphy's Law: Vicious lawsuits won't happen if we don't put up with them. Victims and innocent citizens have been taking a beating for too long, and now—hands raised—we're ready to SLAPP back.

Twenty-two

Cleaning Up the Dirt

THE PUBLIC HAS HAD ITS FILL OF DIRTY TRICKS, LAW-yers who cheat, and judges who denigrate and compound the suffering of innocent crime victims.

When an attorney hides behind a license or a judge hides behind a robe as an excuse to behave badly, he or she should be shamed out of the system. The law is supposed to help keep us civilized. When the professionals in charge of the law act like idiots, civilization itself takes a hit.

Part of the problem lies in the gap between our expecta-tions and the sometimes sordid realities of justice. Lawyers and judges do their thing in wood-paneled courtrooms, adorned with sepia-toned pictures of important-looking men who are no doubt long dead. Pomp and circumstance practically oozes out of the walls. The high priests of the court speak Latin, cite cases from dusty law books, and utter multisyllabic mumbo jumbo like "heretofore the party of the first part," blah, blah, and blah. The judges sit wrapped in flowing black robes, delivering life-altering pronouncements from on high. For most people, this is at least a little bit awe inspiring and intimidating. So our expectations are raised that this is serious business and real justice will be done. Too often, the public's expectations are dashed by bad outcomes.

With more than a few bad apples and an increasing degree of public exposure because of 24/7 news—and, of course, the public's apparently insatiable appetite for things controversial—judges and lawyers are on the hot seat in the court of public opinion. Maybe the bright light of publicity will serve as a kind of quality control device, and things will get better. I certainly hope so.

With so many lawyers and judges making the news for the horrible things they do, it's no wonder people pay no attention to the ones who are doing good work and going out of their way to honor their profession. Let me take a moment to do just that. Many judges spend their nights and weekends teaching, talking to community groups, helping mentor new judges, and working with high school, college, and law school students on mock trial competitions. Lots of lawyers volunteer their time developing civilized justice systems in underdeveloped countries, in many cases representing poor battered women who are forced to choose between being beaten by their husbands and homelessness.

Lawyers regularly donate their time to provide free legal advice and to make house calls to draft wills for the elderly and the disabled. In fact, the good deeds of lawyers are all over the place, but we don't see them, in large part because the bad apples are hogging all the press attention.

As I previously mentioned, jokes about the legal system used to bug me, but not anymore. Joke away, American public, and don't stop until the people in charge start getting it right.

What does that mean? Getting it right means making sure that justice, not winning, is the name of the game.

Getting it right means making sure lawyers who engage in dirty tricks are punished and those who lie to get guilty criminals off are disbarred the first time they do it.

Getting it right means making sure lawyers do not become judges if they intend to use the power of the robe to promote an improper agenda. We understand this when a new judge is appointed to the United States Supreme Court. Well, we now need to extend this same concern to cover the judges who preside over the cases that influence our daily lives, and directly affect the safety of our communities.

Getting it right means finding a way to make fighting for victims a financially valuable endeavor, especially in light of the millions of tax dollars we waste every year helping obviously guilty murderers file frivolous appeals to challenge perfectly valid convictions. I'm not suggesting spending any less on regular appellate proceedings—or even unusual appeals decades after the fact, which legitimately press claims of actual innocence—but shouldn't we at least try to save a few bucks by heading off completely bogus legal proceedings?

Finally, getting it right means encouraging lawyers to do more pro bono work so that the profession as a whole rediscovers the importance of not always thinking about the profit margin. Yes, we lawyers have a right to make a living—even a good living—but we have an obligation and the capacity to do so much more.

You can find lawyers willing to make things better in every corner of this country, in both small towns and big cities and in federal courtrooms as well as community centers where minor traffic violations are resolved. I try to do my part by representing victims in civil lawsuits for money, and by turning away lots of cases where I could make even more money, because I want to be sure I have time to do pro bono work. It's not that I don't like the profit side of lawyering, or that I couldn't try to make victims pay for my work. I could, and in fact, a few do. But I just can't get my head around the idea that I should send a bill to someone who's already suffered at the hands of a criminal. It's bad enough when people are hurt by violence. They should not also be forced to shell out money for a lawyer to make sure the justice system doesn't beat them up some more.

Much of what I do for victims isn't easy, and some of it makes judges (and certainly some lawyers) crazy. I've been accused of butting in where I don't belong. I've been called a troublemaker, and worse. One judge hissed at me when I was giving a talk at a judicial training event. I asked a nearby judge to slap her for me. But a lot of lawyers and judges thank me for what I do. They know what's going on. They see the problems. They're frustrated, too, and they appreciate that I call it like I see it.

Much of what I do for victims also isn't taught in law school. This means if I can't find a form in the back of the law books to cover how I'm supposed to handle an issue—which is almost always the case—I make it up. If I can't find a constitutional provision that applies to my client's situation, I stomp my feet and cite the inherent power of the court. Sometimes it works.

I understand that the criminal justice system is not supposed to be a day at the beach for victims. On the other hand, it's not supposed to cause extra suffering, either. It's supposed to be fair. When bad things happen needlessly to victims, it's not only about one person feeling gypped or uncomfortable. It's about an entire system malfunctioning, and it's about the audacity of the people in charge calling it justice. The reputation of our criminal courts has been faltering since the O. J. Simpson trial, and unless major changes are implemented soon, respect for the system will continue to hover around the edges of the hopper. This is unacceptable for a nation that prides itself as a world leader, whose government is founded on principles of fundamental respect for the equal rights of all citizens.

The law as an institution is far more important than any single person, lawyer, judge, or corporation. When the law works the way it should, it helps us treat one another with civility. This is a good thing. When it fails, we lose the value of these essential ideals, which is why you have a right—no, a duty—to complain when you see an injustice. Scream! Throw things! Make as much noise as possible until the people in charge get it right. If you're not fighting to make it better, you're part of the problem.

This book has given you a few ideas about how to make

things better, but it is by no means the final word on how to fix what's broken. You, the reader, have to come up with your own ideas. You have to find and join forces with like-minded others to demand change. There is great power in numbers.

Use the Internet to communicate and brainstorm with people across the country. Create a volunteer group in your neighborhood. Give money to worthy advocates who are doing meaningful work. Put ads in local papers. Sponsor community education events, and get yourself on local or national television to talk about the injustices that you see.

Contact elected officials. Organize a rally. Write letters to judges. Submit op-eds to newspapers. Make a protest sign and stand in front of your statehouse, courthouse, or town hall every day until someone in a position to do something pays attention.

As I've said to many, many audiences composed of angry citizens fed up with injustice: Do something—anything! Do not wait for a disaster, and don't expect an invitation. Inject yourself into the process, demand a seat at the table, let your voice be heard, and then do not stop speaking until you are satisfied that there is truly justice for all.

ACKNOWLEDGMENTS

Writing this book was hard but figuring out who to name in the acknowledgments section was impossible. Thus, at the risk of sounding philosophical about who deserves recognition for being an inspirational part of this book, I am opting for the all-inclusive "you know who you are" technique, with special attention paid only to my children. Each of them suffered, and I hope will someday benefit, not only because of what it took to write this book but also because of the way my lifetime commitment to justice for crime victims has sometimes deprived them of my attention.

I'm also grateful to the people who read this book in its various stages and offered helpful feedback. My husband, Rick, and my friends Lynne, Arthur, Susan, Dawna, Geej, and Angela all gave time they didn't have. Judge Roderick Kennedy found a way to use poetry to nudge me away from needless hyperbole, and my sister, Barbara, one of the busiest and most dedicated mothers I know, managed to read it and give good advice between carpools, doctor visits, and helping her children get pudding out of the dog's ear.

A special note of thanks to Bill O'Reilly, whose support over the past decade has made all the difference. We don't agree about everything, but we share a commitment to the protection of children and an abiding faith that Americans, like no other culture, can transcend political differences in a common quest for a better society.

Pundits and talk show hosts are a funny breed. People take us seriously—and to be honest, I never say something on television that I don't believe is true (though I might ham it up a little for effect). But let me let you in on a little secret: we know that ratings matter and we know what works on television. This doesn't mean we're not sincere, but it means you're only getting a small piece of who we really are when you hear us pontificating about an issue. I wish I could use my airtime to tell you about all the things that I fight for, all the cases I volunteer to work on when nobody is looking and that raise important issues about justice and fair treatment for victimized women, men, and children. But I don't own a network.

Even this book is but a slice of the pie. But it's a bigger slice than the typical television sound bite. Important issues worthy of attention are not covered, and I apologize for that. For example, the family court system is a mess, and I hear stories every day, mostly from mothers but from a few fathers, too. Parents like Wendy Titelman (whose case should have made headlines) who love their children more than life itself but have been forbidden to have any contact with them as punishment for being "too protective." I could have written an entire book on the dirty tricks that go on in our family courts.

And I could have written about the atrocities going on in the legal world of child protective services. I can't even keep up with the e-mail and phone messages I receive about children "falling through the cracks," some literally dying, while under the care of a state agency. Many social workers are deeply committed, and more resources are needed. But the problems run deeper than that. All the money in the world didn't help little Haleigh Poutre, a Massachusetts child who nearly died in 2005 after she was beaten by her adoptive mother. (I represent her biological mother.) Social services ignored more than a dozen reports of abuse and claimed they responded appropriately because they were told the child was self-abusive. Wouldn't any respectable social worker know that's what abusive parents say when they're trying not to get caught? Again, I could have written a whole book on the failure of child protective service agencies in this country.

I limited the book's scope to the criminal justice system, and even then I had to leave a lot of things out. So I want to hear what you think about what's in here and what's missing.

There might be a sequel and your ideas could be featured. The *Justice for Some* Web site is set up so that you can have a say. Join me there so we can talk about what matters to you and how we can work together to build a better legal system—one that promises *and* delivers Justice for All.

Index

267

Index